To Marjorie
Dona L
2002

# The History of Clarksburg, King's Valley, Purdum, Browningsville and Lewisdale

by

Dona L. Cuttler

Louisa E. Etters ©2001

Heritage Books, Inc.

Other Heritage Books by the author:

***The History of Hyattstown***
***The History of Comus***
***The History of Barnsville and Sellman***
***The History of Dickerson, Mouth of Monacacy,***
***Oakland Mills, and Sugarloaf Mountain***
***Montgomery Circuit Court Records, 1788-1988***
***The History of Poolesville***
***The Genealogical Companion to***
***Rural Montgomery Cemeteries***

**Original artwork by**
**Louise Ehlers**

**Published 2001 by**

**HERITAGE BOOKS, INC.**
**1540E Pointer Ridge Place**
**Bowie, Maryland 20716**

**1-800-398-7709**
**www.heritagebooks.com**

**ISBN 0-7884-1852-1**

*Dedicated to*
*The Memory of*
*Joy Julia Beall McCallum*
*March 4, 1957 - January 6, 2001*

## Acknowledgments

Many individuals have assisted me during this project. I wish to thank them for collecting data, verifying information, legwork, accommodations, and pointing me in the right direction. Bernardine Gladhill Beall served as the facilitator during this project. She escorted me, housed me, connected me and advise me. Michael F. Dwyer prepared the way with research and photographs of locations no longer accessible. I am indebted to him, again. Mary Wolfe Hertel assisted with legwork and documents. Mary Lou Beall Ballew, Eloise Haney Woodfield, Thomas L. Woodfield, Ritchie Lee Haney, Stewart E. Walker III, Jeannie Raines and Joann Woodson contacted individuals which I would never have met so that I could interview them, and uncovered material for me to use. They were more generous than I could have hoped for and filled in many gaps. Reverend Lynn Glassbrook allowed access to the materials housed in the Clarksburg United Methodist Church and provided a place for us to work together. Louise Ehlers created the sketch, maps and cover art work. I also wish to thank Elizabeth Miles Burdette, Henry Miles, Jack and Mary Beth McDonough for their contributions and support during the project. To all of you, thank you for making this as accurate and complete as possible.

## Table of Contents

# Photographic Credits


| | | |
|---|---|---|
| Clarksburg 1812 | Montgomery County Historical Society | 3 |
| Tavern in 1812 | Montgomery County Historical Society | 3 |
| Road Crew 1907 | Collection of Clarksburg UMC | 6 |
| Main Street in Clarksburg | Russell V. Lewis | 8 |
| Clarksburg Band | Collection of Joann Woodson | 10 |
| Church of God | Dona Cuttler | 11 |
| Paul Burner House | Dona Cuttler | 13 |
| Frank Soper House | Dona Cuttler | 14 |
| Wilhide House | Dona Cuttler | 15 |
| Soper House | Dona Cuttler | 16 |
| Hurley House | Dona Cuttler | 17 |
| Leaman House | Dona Cuttler | 18 |
| Parsonage | Dona Cuttler | 19 |
| Dronenburg House | Dona Cuttler | 20 |
| Miles-Cecil House | Collection of Michael F. Dwyer | 21 |
| M. E. South Parsonage | Collection of Clarksburg UMC | 22 |
| M. E. South Church | Collection of Clarksburg UMC | 24 |
| Old Parsonage | Dona Cuttler | 25 |
| Store and Post Office | Michael F. Dwyer | 26 |
| Interior of Store | Collection of Gloria King Winter | 27 |
| Store Ledger | Dona Cuttler | 27 |
| Willson House | Dona Cuttler | 29 |
| Barr's Store | Dona Cuttler | 30 |
| Sibley House | Montgomery County Historical Society | 31 |
| Day House | Dona Cuttler | 32 |
| Clarksburg Academy | Collection of Ann Cecil Morrison | 33 |
| King Farm | Collection of Gloria King Winter | 34 |
| Larman's Store | Collection of Gloria King Winter | 35 |
| Wims House | Dona Cuttler | 36 |
| Watkins Store | Collection of Jean Marks | 37 |
| Watkins House | Collection of Jean Marks | 38 |
| Bill Wims House | Collection of Wilson Wims | 39 |
| John Wesley Methodist | Dona Cuttler | 40 |
| School Children | Collection of Virginia Hackey Gray | 45 |
| School Children | Collection of Virginia Hackey Gray | 46 |
| Dowden's Ordinary | Collection of Gloria King Winter | 47 |
| Dowden's Ordinary | Montgomery County Historical Society | 48 |
| Marker | Montgomery County Historical Society | 49 |
| Hammer Hill | Dona Cuttler | 50 |
| King House | Dona Cuttler | 51 |
| Murphy House | Collection of Gloria King Winter | 52 |
| Hilton's Store | Collection of Louisa Lewis Magruder | 53 |
| Miles House | Dona Cuttler | 54 |
| Clarksburg School | Collection of Alice Leighton Schmidt | 55 |
| Students | Collection of Elizabeth Miles Burdette | 56 |
| Students | Collection of Gloria King Winter | 56 |

# History of Clarksburg

Before other settlers came to the area that is now Clarksburg, William Clarke of Lancaster, Pennsylvania drove his wagon regularly to the present-day intersection of Route 121 and Frederick Road to trade goods for furs. Later, William and his son John Clarke, Sr. were privates in the 6th Co. of Major Gist's Maryland 400. Both men were mustered out in August of 1757. William died in Harford County, Maryland.

Frederick Road has also been known as The Georgetown Road and The Great Road. From the mid-1730's to the mid-1750's few men of European descent were in this vicinity, and the area was Queen Caroline Parish, part of Prince George's County. From 1748 until 1776 Clarksburg was part of Frederick County. As Frederick Town grew the "Great Road" saw more traffic and Clarke set up a trading post. Michael Ashford Dowden's establishment was under construction for about a year beginning in the spring of 1753 and it opened for business in July of 1754. In August of that year, he received a license for keeping a public house—a house on a public road opened to travelers. Along the Great Road were various taverns for travelers and locals. Dowden's Ordinary was one of the oldest taverns in the vicinity. Many notable men stopped here for a night's lodging and meetings convened here also. General Braddock and his men camped here April 15-17, 1755.

The land that became Clarksburg was previously part of a land grant to Lord Calvert. Tracts were patented between 1740 and 1793 in the area. The first such tract was "Belt's Tomahawk" for 150 acres to Jeremiah Belt in 1740. Following that were: "Warfield's Vineyard" to Alexander Warfield in 1745 for 270 acres; "Luck's All" 64 acres surveyed for Michael Dowden in 1748; "Hammer Hill" 40 acres surveyed for Michael Dowden; "Benton's Lot" 50 acres surveyed for Joseph Benton in 1750; "Black Oak Thicket" 50 acres surveyed for Michael Dowden; "Pleasant Plains" 100 acres surveyed for Thomas Hinton in 1754; "Cow Pasture" 3, 854 acres surveyed for Henry Griffith on February 10, 1761; "Hickory Thickett" 50 acres surveyed for Robert Peter in 1762; "Timber Neck" 60 acres surveyed for Richard Waters in 1764; "Dorsetshire" 740 acres surveyed for William Sargent in 1764; "Belt's Addition" 43 acres surveyed for John Belt; "Garnkirk" 1,803 acres surveyed for Robert Peter in 1787 which included "The Grange," "Burdette's Force Put," "Hickory Thicket," "White Oak Bottom," and part of "Luck's All." In 1789 "Easy Come By" a 7 acre tract, was surveyed for John Clarke. In 1792 part of "Dorsetshire" was resurveyed as "Ebenezer" the 315 acre tract from which the local Methodist Church took it's first name. John Clark patented the tract and then donated a portion for the meeting house. In 1793 John Belt had "Woodport" patented. This property became the land that was divided into lots for the village of Clarksburg.

In 1776 one of the first acts of the new government was dividing Frederick County. The lower portion became Montgomery County, named for patriot Richard Montgomery. Clarksburg became the Second Election District in Montgomery County, which included: Hyattstown, Damascus, Cedar Grove, Browningsville, Boyds, and Gaithersburg. Damascus, Cedar Grove and Gaithersburg were later separate districts.

The Great Road, previously called 240, currently designated Route 355, led from Washington to Frederick. Clarksburg is 30 miles from Washington and 15 miles from Frederick. This made it a convenient coach stop as it was a days journey to the Capital

City. General Edward Braddock and his troops traveled this road in April of 1755 enroute to Frederick, before going to Pennsylvania. The road was to be maintained by the home owners of each section, and a superviser oversaw the endeavor. It was supposed to be two-rails across, or twenty-two feet, to allow coaches and wagons to pass each other safely. But the amount of traffic on the dirt surface left the road in deplorable condition much of the time. Deep ruts were worn by wagon wheels, animals being driven to market, and teams pulling vehicles. Spring rains made some sections dangerous, such as Long Hill and Magruder's Hill.

John G. Clarke, Jr., for whom the town was named, had a house built c. 1781. He was the son of John, and the grandson of William Clarke who had established the trading post. John married Ann Archey and had seven children, the eldest, Sarah Jupine Clark married William Willson in 1797. Their son, Leonidas Willson, and his wife Maria Harris Willson later lived in this first house. Leonidas was the propritor of the oldest store which by 1879 was conducted by Lewis and Williams.

In the early 1790's John G. Clarke, Jr. surveyed the town and laid it out in lots for homes and businesses. He was appointed the first Justice of the Peace on April 6, 1798, elected a County Comissioner in 1799, and appointed the first postmaster in March of 1800. The post office was named Clarksburgh, but the "h" was later dropped. John was a private in the Sixth Company of Major Gist's Maryland Four Hundred. He was one of the founders of the Methodist Episcopal Church in Clarksburg and was buried in the Clarke Family Cemetery.

Jeremiah Belt was an Indian Scout for the Colonial government. In 1748 Captain George Beall formed a militia company. Among the horse troop was Thomas Dowden, Michael Dowden, John Dowden, William Beall, Edward Buscey, Basil Beall, Hilleary Williams, Joseph Williams and George Willson.

The Methodist Meeting of Clarksburg was formed on June 5, 1788. Ebenezer Chapel, a log structure, was built in 1794. By 1853 the brick Greek Revival church was built, but by 1905 the building was in need of major repairs. The congregation opted to have the brick church demolished and replace it with a frame structure which was completed in 1907. The Methodist Episcopal South Church was constructed in 1871 and later served as the hall after the two churches united in 1939. The Pleasant Plains Church was constructed when the African American Methodist members formed their own circuit. The Boyd Charge included what is now the John Wesley Methodist Church built in 1878. On April 1, 1800 a post office was established in Clarksburg. Within Montgomery County, only Rockville's post office is older, being established in 1795. Mail arrived on the stagecoach, or sometimes via special messengers on horseback. On August 25, 1814 Captain John Brengle's Company marched to Clarksburg enroute to the Battle of North Point.

The town was laid out along the Frederick Road, one of the early post-roads. The road was used as the stagecoach line from Frederick to Georgetown and it remains as the present main street through Clarksburg. As other land was purchased in the vicinity small communities developed outside the town. John Duckett King's area became King's Valley, and Stringtown emerged southeast of town. The soil was fertile in some areas which produced wheat, corn, oats, tobacco, hay and potatoes. But in the hollow and rocky areas other industry sprang up such as saw mills, a distillery, and smithys. One of the

1812 Sketch of Clarksburg

**1812 sketch of the Tavern**

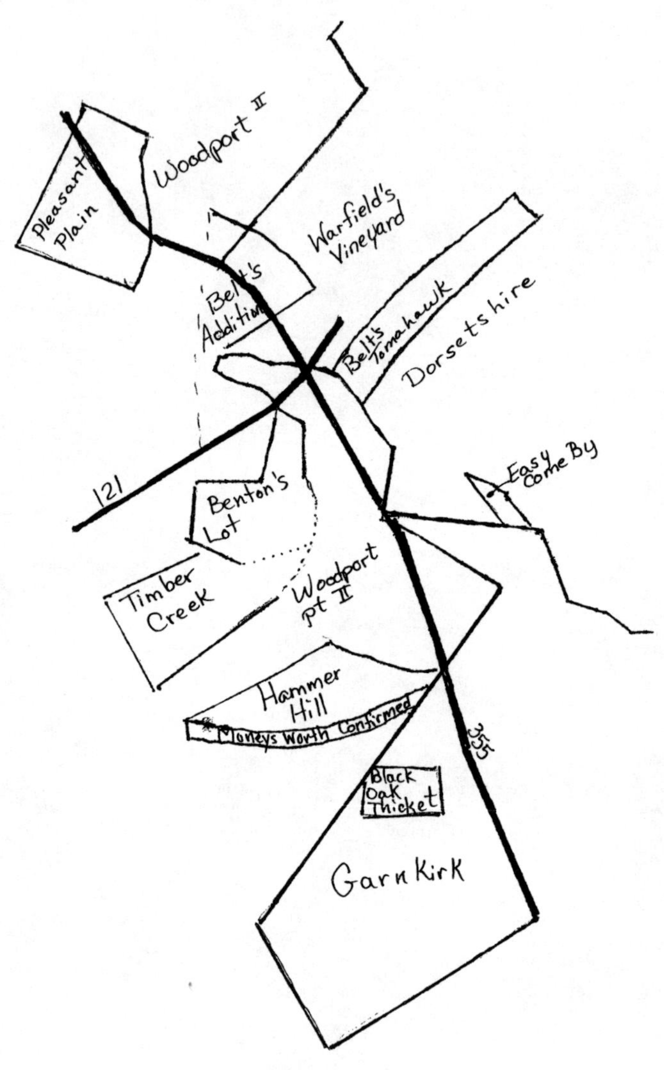


**Land Tracts in Clarksburg and vicinity**

merchants from 1842-1849 was George W. Mobley. James E. Williams operated a mercantile business from 1860-1865.

The Clarksburg Lodge No., 100 of the International Order of Odd Fellows was instituted on August 28, 1858. They subsequently met in a hall which was purchased from Charles R. Murphy in 1871.

Union troops passed through Clarksburg in June of 1861 as they marched from Rockville en route to Harper's Ferry. In September of 1862 General George B. McClellan's men traveled the Great Road from Washington City to Frederick in pursuit of General Robert E. Lee's column. The cavalry hurried by on September 6th, and Major General Edwin V. Sumner's men arrived on the 10th. They left on the 11th and McClellan departed on the 12th after receiving a telegram from President Lincoln inquiring of the situation.

Sporadic troop movements continued through Clarksburg due to it's location along a major artery. In July of 1864 following the Battle of the Monocacy, Major General Jubal Early's Confederate troops marched through Clarksburg en route to Washington on July 10th. But the largest encampment came in October of that year when Lieutenant Colonel Napoleon B. Knight of the 1st Delaware Cavalry arrived on the 19th and the following day they were joined by Smith's Independent Maryland Company of Calvary. Their assignment was to locate any of Mosby's Rangers, and then to guard the banks of the Potomac River. To accomplish this second command they relocated closer to the river.

In 1879 the Clarksburg was the third most populous village in Montgomery County, behind Rockville and Poolesville. That same year the Baltimore and Ohio Railroad began train service at Boyd's Station, just four miles from Clarksburg. The Clarksburg Literary Association was established in 1879. The president was Judge Charles Richardson Murphy. William R. Windsor was the Vice President, John S. Belt the treasurer, Thomas H. S. Boyd coresponding secretary, and Thomas A. Burdette recording secretary. The purpose of the association was to encourage the reading of good literature and for compiling local history.

Mahlon T. Lewis of Clarksburg propagated bees, and raised honey bees. Using a device that was new at the time, he had the combs suctioned out. In this way the cobs were undamaged and could be replaced in the hive for the bees to refill. For a two hundred fifty dollar investment in bees and equipment, profit averaged one thousand dollars annually, in the 1880's.

Peach orchards yielded about one hundred dollars per acre in the 1880's. The first three years of the tree's life were tedious, and fruit bearing began the fourth year. Most varieties grown in the area matured in August, but a few were harvested in September.

The road plat for the road from Clarksburg to Browningsville was plated in 1885. The following were paid for damages or expenses: S. A. Richards, $80.00; John N. Soper and brothers, $275.00; James S. Buxton, $125.00; Leonidas Willson, $200.00; John P. Lawson, $90.00; Obediah S. Layton, $10.00; James Wilkerson Day, $10.00; Annie Robertson, $200.00; John P. Sellman, 3 day examiner $6.00; John C. Lyddard, 3 day examiner $6.00; William Williams, 2 day $4.00; R. W. Benton, chainman 1 day $1.25; G. S. Stone, chainman $1.25; Benjamin F. Hawkins, $1.25; Richard H. Bowman, rodman $1.25; C. F. Townsend, surveyor $8.00.

Clarksburg was incorporated in 1892. It had street lights and sidewalks. In 1937 the incorporation was withdrawn.

The Great Road was finally graded and paved in 1907. Building the road gave many locals employment, including Lee Day who is pictured below. Modern equipment was not available so the work was done manually.

Road crew in 1907

On August 28, 1954 "Clarksburg Day" was held to celebrate the 200th Anniversary of Dowden's Ordinary. A flier from the occasion lists local merchants, and the town slogan "An Old Community with New Ideas." Some of the merchants which advertised in the flier were: Whipp's Garage - Sinclair Service Station; Barr's Grocery; Garnkirk Gardens; The Chicken Shop and Brady-Roetteis Lumber.

Interstate 70 S, later called I-270 brought increased traffic to Clarksburg. As Comsat and other corporations spralled north from Washington, D. C., bedroom communities began to spring up in the vicinity. Several of the older homes were removed to make way for 'progress.'

After meeting in a house across from the Post Office for several years, the Green Ridge Baptist Church was built in 1972. It is located on 355 just north of town. Clarksburg also has a Church of God.

In June of 2000 plans were announced to extend Stringtown Road and redesign the I-270 interchange for Clarksburg. Stringtown was named for the members of the string band that lived along the road. Foreman's hill is the area closer to Clarksburg, so named for the family that inhabited that area. A 250th anniversary of Dowden's Ordinary is planned for 2002.

## Clarksburg in 1880

William H. Buxton, Postmaster
John S. Belt, Justice Of The Peace
John H. Gibson, merchant
Lewis & Williams, merchants
Thomas K. Galloway, physician
Richard H. Thompson, physician
William A. Waters, physician
James B. Neel, tax collector
H. A. Gaver, Minister, M. E. South Church
Randolph Richardson Murphy, Minister, M. E. Church
Lewis Housen, tailor
Leonidas Willson, miller
Luther Green King, distiller and miller
Thomas H. Stockton Boyd, publisher
John W. Hurley, shoemaker
Robert S. Hilton, tobacco inspector
Charles Thomas Anderson, wheelwright
William W. Dronenburg, blacksmith
William J. Dronenburg, blacksmith
Richard A. Leaman, blacksmith
Leonard Dent Shaw, blacksmith
Wilson L. Soper, U. S. Mail Carrier

Postal Patrons
Caleb Beall
John S. Belt
Elizabeth Boyd
John W. Byrne
Edward N. Darby
Nathan Darby
James Wilkerson Day
William J. Dronenburg
George W. Hilton
Joseph Henry Clay Hoyle
George W. Israel
James T. Johnson
James S. Kemp
Charles M. King
Edward J. King
Rufus Fillmore King
Obediah S. Layton
Edward Lewis
H. A. Gaver
John A. Lewis
Gassaway W. Linthicum
James H. Miles
Charles Richard Murphy
James H. Purdum
Abraham H. Rose
S. L. Rose
Cephas Summers
Zadoc Summers
Samuel C. Thompson
Andrew J. Waters
Edward H. Waters
Dr. William A. Waters
William Watkins
William Williams
William L. Williams
William R. Windsor
Richard Leaman
Leonard Dent Shaw
Randolph Richardson Murphy

## Postmasters of Clarksburg

| | |
|---|---|
| John Clarke | April 1, 1800 in Clarke's Trading Post |
| William Willson of John | June 10, 1837 |
| George Moberly | September 23, 1842 |
| Leonidas Willson | July 19, 1848 |
| Z. J. H. W. Burditt | July 22, 1849 |
| George W. Hilton | December 9, 1857, in Hilton's store |
| Leo W. Reid | June, 29, 1861 |
| Reuben A. Hurley | June 18, 1862 |
| George W. Hilton | December 3, 1863, in Hilton's store |
| Mary L. Power | March 30, 1865, in the Power house |
| John H. Gibson | April 1, 1873, in the Gibson store |
| William H. Buxton | November 10, 1875 |
| Robert S. Hilton | October 28, 1885, in Hilton's store |
| William H. Buxton | March 16, 1898 |
| Charles S. Hilton | March 26, 1901, in Hilton's store |
| William Edward Lewis | June 30, 1911 |
| Levi Price | May 12, 1914 |
| Lois Irene Holland | June 15, 1918 |
| Lois Irene H. Maxwell | June 8, 1919 |
| Clifton Dronenburg | September 24, 1923 |
| Edith Lillian Purdum Barr | September 25, 1925 |
| Mary N. Haupin | November 1, 1949 |
| Julia M. Hess | January 6, 1950 |
| Ora Henning King | April 25, 1963 opened the U. S. Post Office |
| Donald Kersey | October, 1968 |
| C. Miller Day | May 1, 1971 |
| Dan Albert | October 1, 1980 |

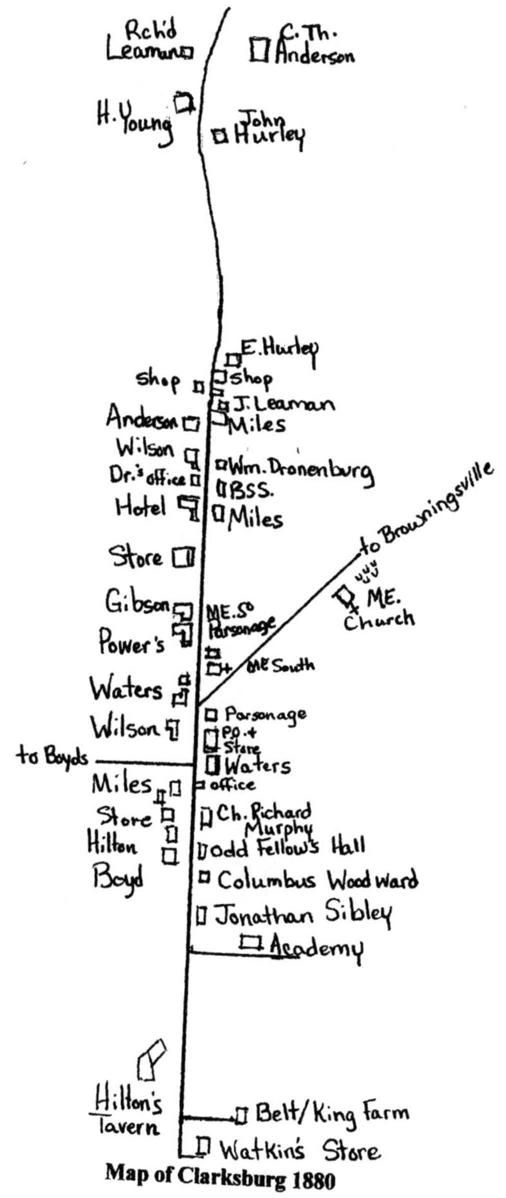


**Map of Clarksburg 1880**

Clarksburg's Brass Band

The band was organized by James Mortimer Hurley, son of William Levi and Elizabeth Hurley. Their other sons John, Alexander and George were also members of the band. The band played for a variety of occasions from fairs to parades to picnics. Many other communities also had brass bands; among them, Browningsville, Hyattstown, Germantown, and Poolesville. This photograph was taken c. 1875 in front of Mary Mile's (later Cecil's) and shows how high the wagon wheels were to survive the road conditions. Professor J. Mortimer Hurley is sporting the stove pipe hat near the center of the picture. Other members included Luther Green King, and the Lewises, Purdums, Greens and Dronenburgs. The band members practiced on Saturday nights at the Hurley house, and sometimes in an outbuilding behind Willie J. Dronenburg's house. Professor Hurley taught clarinet, flute, bass horn and guitar lessons. The other instruments pictured are trombone, coronet, long horn, and bass drum. Members of the band performed in suits, not uniforms, and usually had 12 members at their concerts. "The Clarksburg March," composed by Hurley, was one of the numbers included in their performances.

## Little Bennett Park

Little Bennett Park was designed to preserve the watershed for the Little Bennett Creek. Plans were announced in 1963 and the Maryland National Capital Park and Planning Commission began acquiring land soon afterward. Within park boundries some houses were demolished or burned once they were acquired because they did not meet county codes. The lane to Hanson Miles house, which had burned in 1940, became Hammond Drive after Bill Hammond ran a barrell stave mill where he housed workers in used World War II dwellings. One well and one privy was built for every three or four homes. The former Church of God is the only building from the community now standing. Begun by William Tucker, the church built a new facility on Clarksburg Road and the old building is now used as the nature center and store in Little Bennett Park.

The John Ashton house was an example of the older houses which are now gone. Located approximately half of a mile up the hill from the Kingsley School, the house sat on the left side of the road. On a neighboring hill sat the home of Charlie Piquett. The Loys also had a home in this vicinity. Lee Wilson was a saw mill operator who had a home in this area. The site of the saw mill is designated by a sign on Clarksburg Road near Kingsley. Other houses remained in the family for a designated period of time such as the homes of Warner Wims, James Henry and Altia Wims, Oscar and Mary Hackey, Marshall and Irene Day, Robert and Jessie Gray, Stella Marshall, Dominic Naples, Huertas, and Runyons. Across from the Wims farm was a ball field where the Wildcats played their games. Park plans once called for a lake in this meadow, but the field remains.

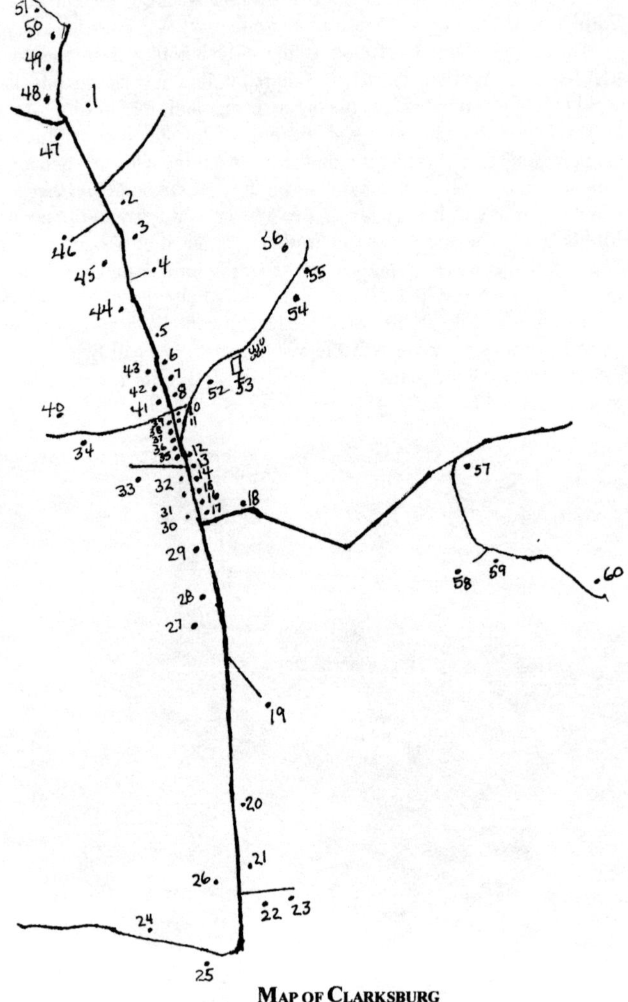


**Map of Clarksburg**

## Residences and Businesses of Clarksburg

1. Paul Burner House

This two-story brick house was built in 1946 for Paul F. and Neva Thompson Burner. It is three bay by two bay with a gable roof and brick exterior chimney. When land was being purchased for Little Bennett Park, the Beechers were living in a house that was bought and they were moved here. Then the plans called for this land to be part of the park, too. Instead of moving them again, they were granted an easement, and remained here. Presently Henry and Isabel Hamm live in this house.

2. Frank Soper House

Built for William Franklin Soper in 1933 by Floyd Grimes, this two-story two bay by two bay frame house is typical of the period in which it was constructed. It has a full-length front porch and six rooms. The front porch roof is supported by tapered square colomns on brick piers and the balustrade has an interesting geometric pattern. Next door was the site of Charles Thomas Anderson's wheelwright shop. In 1865 Nicholas Worthington sold Charles Thomas Anderson and by 1870 Anderson was making butter churns at this location. He was also a successful carriage maker and wheel wright. He patented several inventions. In the winter the steps and retaining wall are still visible.

3. Wilhide House

George and Mary Wilhide had this house built in the late 1940's and ran a business here frying chickens. The Wilhide Chicken Shop was operated in the 1940's and 50's and many picnicers carried tasty meals up to Sugarloaf Mountain. Phoebe Chaney Dorsey worked here for many years, cooking and serving crispy fried chicken. Subsequent owners include V. I. Queen, and Rosalie B. Willis. The Wilhide's son Raymond and wife Alice lived in a house on the adjoining property. Both are parcels of "Wood Port".

4. Soper House

The property for this farm was purchased by William C. Soper on August 31, 1829. The present two-story frame house was built for William Oscar Soper and wife Mary Somerville Duvall Soper c. 1903. The house is three bay by one bay with a gable roof and center gable facade. There is a central brick chimney. One of the unusual features is the two over two long widows. He huckstered produce grown on local farms, including Garrett Cooley's Store. Soper also operated a successful business in the Washington Market. The property is a parcel of "Wood Port".

5. William Hurley House

The original section of this one-and-a-half story frame house was built for Arnold Warfield c. 1801 and is rumored to have been the first voting place in Clarksburg. It was purchased by Obed Hurley in 1835 who sold it to Judge William Levi Hurley in 1842. The smaller building first housed workers and has a basement. The present structure was built around the log section at this time. It is a two bay by one bay two-story house with an exterior and interior chimney. William Hurley used the one-story building as a shoe shop during this period. The local tannery produced leather, and Hurley was Clarksburg's leading shoemaker for over 30 years. In 1845 James Mortimer Hurley organized the Clarksburg Brass Band and wrote the Clarksburg March. He gave instrumental instruction here, as did his nephew Parke Buxton, the organist. After William's death in 1878 his widow Elizabeth continued to live here with their daughters Helen Hurley and Josephine S. Hurley Humrichouse who ran a millinery shop in the front room of the house. Later John W. and Frances Marian Richardson Hurley lived here. Their daughter Lydia married William E. Crutchley and lived here with their family.

6. Leaman House

The original log section of the house was probably built for Thomas Kirk who sold it c. 1801 to Arnold Warfield. William King purchased the property in 1807 for $100. Peter Sowers purchased the house in 1814 and sold it to Aquilla Burnsides in who sold it in 1818 to Wattee Williams. Williams was a local carpenter who undoubtedly built some of the other Clarksburg homes. His property was surrounded by a blacksmith, a shoemaker, and the hotel across the street. Thomas Nicholls purchased the property in 1853 for $130 who went into the mercantile business with John H. Gibson. The log house was sold to John Williams, Jr. in 1858 for $350, who in turn sold it to Dr. Rezin R. Thompson in 1866. In 1871 the house was sold to John S. Leaman, also a carpenter who made coffin's, cabinets and furniture. He had a small shop next to the house. In 1890 he built the rear frame addition. Leaman's widow, Elizabeth A. Watkins Leaman and her daughter had the Victorian section added c. 1890. Ella Holland was a seamstress and lived here with her daughter Lois Irene Holland. Lois was the Clarksburg Post Master from 1918 to 1923. In 1961 the property was sold out of the family, and Wilbert T. and H. B. Duncan were subsequent owners.

7. Parsonage

Rufus Howard lived here in 1865 and the house was torn down to make room for the Methodist Episcopal Parsonage. The land was donated to the Trustees by Sarah C. Hilton in 1914. This American Four Square two-story house was built to replace the old parsonage which was sold to Levi Price. Thomas Davis was the first pastor to live here. Rev. W. D. Shindle lived here while serving the Bethesda Methodist Church at Browningsville before they built their own parsonage. Other pastors included Walter Jones, Frank Jaggers, Wallace Brashears, Fred Barnes, and Hartwell Chandler who lived here from 1935 until 1939. Thomas Morgan was the last pastor to live here. In 1941 the United Methodist Church sold the house to Mary M. Lancaster who owned it until 1958. Robert D. Hoffman was a subsequent owner.

8. Dronenburg House

Next to the present gravel lot was Willie Dronenburg's House. He married Margaret A. Rhodes, moved to Clarksburg, and opened his shop in 1850. He purchased this lot across from the hotel in 1853. The two-and-a-half story brick house was built in 1865 and has had several additions which have covered the brick. In 1937 Clifton Dronenburg, grandson of Willie, sold the house and it is now owned by Thomas W. and S. A. Conley. A dentist and craft shop are presently located here. Behind the site of the blacksmith shop was a building where the Clarksburg Band rehearsed on Saturday nights. A nursery sells plants presently in the lot beside the Dronenburg House.

9. Miles - Cecil House

In 1865 Mary A. Burdette lived in the frame one-and-a-half story house. Pictured below is the left section of the house which was log covered in siding. The fence is ornate and unusual for this area. Later this was the home of Mary Ann Shipley Miles whose daughter, Sarah Catherine Miles, married Robert Hilton. By 1880 Hilton is listed as the head of household here. He was a prominent citizen and civic leader for the Clarksburg District. It was during this time that the right section of the house was built. It is visible on page 11 behind the band wagon. During the renovation the porch was removed and the newer section featured two dormers and a Greek Revival style porch. The Cecil family rented the house in the 1920's and lived here for quite a few years. Everett Hammond Cecil, his wife Julia Mae "Mame" Thompson Cecil, and their children moved here from Comus. Their blind daughter Nellie and son Millard "Bub" Cecil were the last of the family living here. Bub is remembered as a clerk in the store and a person that neighborhood children enjoyed playing tricks on. When the intersection was created, the house was demolished. The lot is now the grassy area between Clarksburg Road and the gravel lot. The land was owned by William T. Hannan in 1984.

10. Parsonage for the Methodist Episcopal Church South

This lot of Leonidas Willson's had a log house on it by 1865. In the 1880 census Randolph Richardson Murphy, Minister of the Clarksburg Methodist Episcopal South Church, was residing here prior to the church purchasing the property. The lot was purchased on September 17, 1885 by the Trustees of the Methodist Episcopal Church South for the construction of the circuit parsonage. The Trustees were: Warner W. Welsh, Jr., John A. Lewis, Thomas H. Hoskinson, Wesley A. Maxwell, and James Francis Beall. In 1893 a new fence was put up around the garden and backyard, and a new coal house was built. Also, a fence was built around the entire lot. It was plastered and repainted, the chimney was repaired and the pump was also repaired. The cost for the work was $106.75. In 1896 a new cook stove was purchased. In 1903 the kitchen in the parsonage received a new floor and a coat of paint. The dining room was papered, and several other rooms were carpeted. The value of the parsonage in 1907 was $1,824.00. The property was purchased by Thomas W. Conley in the 1980's. Presently "The Amish Connection" is located here.

11. Methodist Episcopal Church South

This denomination was established in 1865 after a schism in the Methodist Episcopal Church. The Montgomery Circuit included Clarksburg, Hyattstown, Comus, Flint Hill, Forest Grove, Mt. Pleasant [Dickerson], Oak Hill, Beallsville, Thompsontown, and Poolesville. The church was built in 1871 on land which was conveyed by William Waters to the following Trustees: Edward Lewis, John S. Belt, William R. Windsor, John A. Lewis, Warner W. Welsh, John W. Taylor, and Charles Richard Murphy. The annual convention held in Clarksburg took place at Murphy's Grove. In 1879 the convention invited Damascus Order of Templars as the speakers. The Montgomery Circuit was reorganized in 1901 with just five churches for the pastors to take care of. The Clarksburg M. E. South Church was built in 1866. Over the years many renovations took place, as well as maintainance. In 1903 the building was repainted and new steps were built. The Sunday School Superintendant was Wesley Maxwell who travelled from Comus by buggy. Children's Day was an annual, well attended event that showcased the Sunday School education program to the community. Missionary Day was another annual event at which larger than usual collections were taken to support the work of the church. The circuit included 350 square miles with over 400 members in 1895. Included were chapters of the Women's Missionary Society, Epworth Leagues and the Clarksburg Mite Society. This last group met in various homes and presented entertainments, sang hymns and had soirees. During Thomas Morgan's pastorate the two Methodist Churches were reunited. The M. E. South building was then used for a social hall until it was demolished, but the steps are still visible in front of the gazebos on display at "The Amish Connection."

The Pastors for the church were:

| | |
|---|---|
| John P. Hall | 1865-1868 |
| Robert Smith | 1868-1870 |
| F. H. Shipley | 1868-1870 Junior Pastor |
| B. F. Ball | 1870-1872 |
| G. C. Tibbs | 1872-1874 |
| L. L. Lloyd | 1874-1875 |
| William McDonald | 1874-1876 |
| W. Wade | 1876 |
| H. A. Gaver | 1877 |
| James H. Boyd | 1883-1887 Preacher-In-Charge |
| John J. Kahlman | 1885-1886 Junior Preacher |
| Edward L. Geis | 1886-1886 Junior Preacher |
| W. D. Violet | 1886-1886 Junior Preacher |
| David L. Blakemore | 1886-1887 |
| Will G. Hammond | 1887-1890 Preacher-In-Charge |
| William Lee Smith | 1888-1890 |
| A. A. P. Neal | 1890-1891 |
| P. M. Henderson | 1890-1891 |
| A. H. Smith | 1890-1890 |
| William E. Woolf | 1891-1894 |

| | |
|---|---|
| James H. Dulany | 1894-1896 |
| C. D. Smith | 1894-1895 Junior Preacher |
| W. H. D. Sanders | 1896-1900 with H. C. Febrey 1896 and G. W. Bogle, JPs |
| D. L. Reid | 1900-1901 |
| Isaac Gillie Michael | 1901-1905 |
| W. C. Smith | 1905-1906 |
| J. R. Kuchnall | 1906 |
| F. F. Neal | 1907-1908 |
| J. L. Kuhlman | 1907 |
| Harry L. Bivens | 1908-1909 |
| Edward T. Caton | 1909-1910 |
| J. W. Mitchell | 1911-1913 |
| W. C. Smith | 1914-1915 |
| G. R. Mays | 1916-1920 |
| J. D. Pope | 1921-1922 |
| Harry Lewis Coffman | 1922-1926 |
| Julian C. McDonald | 1926-1928 |
| Charles Reiter | 1928-1929 |
| E. Wilson Jordan | 1930-1931 |
| S. J. Dulany | 1932-1937 |
| Thomas Morgan | 1938-1945 |

12. Old Parsonage

The first parsonage for the Montgomery Circuit was built in 1815 on land acquired from Willam Willson. Beverly Waugh was the first circuit preacher to reside here. His records note that individuals paid him between $3.00 and $20.00 for his services for marriage ceremonies. Also in his accounts are the price of earthenware, $2.00; toothbrush and sundries, $1.00; and three yards of cotton, $2.50. On November 7, 1826 the parsonage settlement was made for $2.95. Circuit Riders packed their Bible in their saddle, along with their sermon notes, and rode to one of the churches on the circuit. Sometimes they would take their noon meal with a family and then ride to an afternoon service at another church. In the early days of the Montgomery Circuit there were several churches to lead: Comus, Clarksburg, Goshen, and Hyattstown. In 1904 Rev. Caleb Yost reported that the parsonage needed new steps, a back porch, and the coal house needed a new roof. A new well was dug and Jacob Hager put up a new fence for $61.48. The parsonage was valued at $1,700 at that time. The parsonage received a new coat of paint in 1907. Ira Leamon furnished the material and completed the job for $60.00. The same year the stable was repaired as well as the hen house. The pump was repaired again in 1913. In 1915 the parsonage was sold to Levi and Mary E. Cecil Price. In 1944 Mary Price sold the house and the present owners, Larry T. and Valerie K. Matlock, who purchased it in 1978.

13. Store and Post Office

This was the site of John Clarke's Trading Post. Established April 1, 1800, this was the location of the first post office in Clarksburg, the second oldest in Montgomery County. Mail was carried on the stage and also by post riders, and held at the trading post until area residents came in to town. John Clarke was appointed as the first Postmaster. In 1842 the old trading post building was replaced with a two-story general store. The building was constructed on a fieldstone foundation with a flat roof. William Willson, son-in-law of John Clarke, operated the store until c. 1840. This lot was listed as lot 6 in tax assessments and designated "store house" with the value in 1840 at $205 in 1842 was $1,000. The second section of two-and-a-half stories with a gabled roof was added c. 1860 by Leonidas Willson, son of William and Sarah Jupine Clarke Willson. In 1878 Mary Willson Waters, Leonidas Willson's sister, became a joint owner and operator of the store. The property was purchased by Sarah Isabel Neel Sellman in 1893. In 1914 the store was sold to Levi Price III and his wife Mary E. Cecil Price. The doors were cut into the left section when the Post Office was located here. In 1921 the store was sold to the William Edward Lewis and after Philip Linthicum joined the venture it was operated as Lewis and Linthicum Store. John Edward Lewis purchased the store from his father and at this time the store was covered in red siding and red clapboard. The left half of the store was still log when Emory B. Edwards operated it in the late 1940's. The store closed in 1970 and Roy M. and Pat J. Bradley purchased the property from the Mary Hughes Lewis. C. Miller Day has two leatherbound ledgers from 1827 and 1835 from this store. A zoning amendment will allow the business to open despite the lack of parking facilities, which has kept the store closed for years.

This 1914 photograph shows Levi Price, owner; Edward Lewis and Clifton Darby, clerks; and Edward Cecil, customer. In the lower photograph is one of the store's ledgers. This one is from 1817.

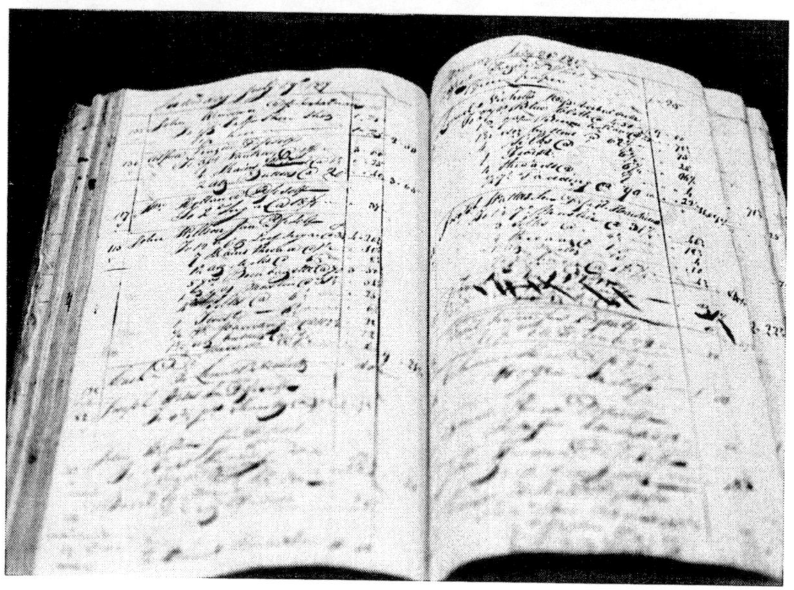

The following excerpts were taken from John Clarke's ledger of 1817:

| | | |
|---|---|---|
| Edward Hughes | posted 3 letters | $1.30 |
| Joseph A. Murphy | 3 1/2 yards of cloth | $5.75 |
| | 1/4 yard plain | $2.75 |
| | 2 1/2 yard Brown Holland | $2.45 |
| | 1 dozen buttons | .62 |
| | 6 thread 1 cent each | .06 |
| Thomas C. Nichols | 2 pair shoes | $2.75 |
| Camden Nichols | cash | |
| Leonard Williams | 2 pair buckskin gloves | .75 |
| John R. Griffith | 2 1 penny nails @ 13 | .26 |
| John Willson (Brother of William Willson) | | |
| | 10 yards of material and a comb | |
| Zadock Magruder bought | 25 yards cambric shirting | $13.75 |
| | 1 4/12 dozen shirt buttons | .25 |
| John Willson of John | 2 jugs | $1.00 |
| William Bennett | cash paid out | $4.22 1/2 |
| Archibald Cecil paid balance on muslin | | .12 |
| Nathan Holland | Bombazette cloth | |
| Samuel Bennett | 1 box candles | .25 |
| Thomas B. Johnson | 1 set of knives and forks | $3.25 |
| Basil Soper | paper of pins | .18 3/4 |
| Horace Waters | ribbons and combs | .8 3/4 |
| Israel Case | paid balance due | |
| John Winemiller | 4 pitchers @ .37 1/2 | $1.50 |
| Samuel Barber | newspapers | .67 1/2 |
| Jane Knott | frequently received .22 cash | |
| Martha Magruder | $4.00 cash | |
| Hezekiah Northcraft | 2 pounds of coffee @ .28 | .56 |
| Greenberry Howard | 1 twist of taobacco @ 6 1/2 | .6 1/2 |
| William Bennett | 235 pounds of beef @ 6 1/2 | $15.27 |
| William Johnson | 500 pounds of pork @ .09 | $45.00 |
| Arthur Dillehay | 2 1/2 yards of muslin | .31 |
| Benjamin Dillehay | 1 thimble | .06 |
| | 1 fur hat | $4.50 |
| Joshua Stewart for his wife | 1 shawl | $1.12 1/2 |
| Thomas B. Johnson | 5 yards plain blue fabric @ .60 | $3.00 |
| | 4 1/2 pounds of cheese @ .20 | .90 |
| | 2 pounds of sugar @ .14 | .28 |
| John Bennett for his wife | 3 pounds of sugar @ .12 1/2 | .37 1/2 |
| | 1 pound of coffee | .25 |
| Elisha Howard | posted a letter | .25 |
| Arthur Dillehay | 4 yards of cord @ .75 | $3.00 |
| Elizabeth McClain | 4 needles @ .05 | .20 |

14. Horace Willson House

The original single-story three-bay rear section was built for Dr. John Reid c. 1800 who sold it to Thomas Anderson in 1813. Dr. Horace Willson purchased the lot and cabin valued at $400 in 1821. Dr. Willson served in the State House of Delegates from 1831-1832 and in the State Senate from 1838-1841 as the only Montgomery County Representative. The one and a half story frame house with two dormers was built for Dr. Horace Willson in the 1840's. In 1843 the house was valued $700. He had his office and medical library in this house which has three interior chimneys, and two gabled dormers. Mary E. L. Willson Neel purchased the house in 1852. After the death of her husband, Thomas Neel, Dr. William Augustus Waters was living here in 1865 and had an office here. Mary married Dr. Waters and they were living here in 1879. The house passed to her daughter Sarah Isabel Neel Sellman in the 1890's. Elwood and Edith Lillian Purdum Barr lived here before selling it in 1966. Henry J. and Jean C. Noyes purchased the house and have had various occupants here.

15. site of the Murphy House, I. O. O. F. Hall and Barr's Store

Charles Richard Murphy lived in a house where the parking lot is now for the Clarksburg Store. He was a tax collector, Judge of the Orphan's Court, and a son of Charles Hill and Julia Ann Richardson Murphy. A blacksmith shop was located between the house and hall. The Clarksburg Lodge No. 100 was instituted on August 28, 1858 with Rufus K. Waters, William R. Windsor, Dr. Richard Thompson, Charles R. Murphy and A. M. Layton as the charter members. The first officer's were: Dr. Richard Thompson, Noble Grand; Rufus K. Waters, Vice-Grand; A. M. Layton, Secretary; and Charles R. Murphy, Treasurer. The building was referred to as Murphy's Hall, as it was purchased from Charles R. Murphy in 1871. The officers in 1880 were George W. Darby, Noble Grand; Nathan H. Darby, Vice Grand; Charles R. Murphy, Secretary; John H. Gibson, Treasurer; William R. Windsor, Past-Grand and John Leaman, O. Grand. During the halcyon days membership reached one hundred fellows. Guilds were first centered around a trade, such as masons. Odd Fellows were all of the men who did not fit into any other trade guild, thus called odd fellows. The Odd Fellow's Hall was rented by the Methodist Church during the construction of their church in 1909. The Murphy house and hall were demolisged prior to construction of the store and parking lot. In 1922 the present one-story block store was built for Sarah Edith Lewis Purdum. In December of 1923 Mrs. Purdum sold the store to Elwood E. & Edith Lillian Purdum Barr. The Post Office was located here until the new Post Office was built next door. In the 1950's Emory B. Edwards was the proprietor of the store. In October of 1966 Henry J. and Jean C. Noyes purchased the store.

16. site of the Columbus Woodward and Jonathan Sibley Houses

The original rear log section was built on a fieldstone foundation perhaps by James Hawkins as early as 1809 when it was valued at $45. Mary Griffith purchased the property in 1814 and lived here until 1829 when the porperty was assessed at $200. The subsequent owners were William Benton, Mary Crandle, Charles Murphy, Obediah Stillwell Layton, George Hilton and in 1879 Columbus Woodward, a local carpenter, who was living here when the Montgomery County Atlas was drawn. In 1889 Singleton Davis purchased the property and Jane Davis sold it in 1892. The two-story frame house with gabled roof was built about the time that John H. Wims, a former slave who settled in Clarksburg, purchased the property. The frame section with the jig saw trim on the porch gave the house a Victorian touch. Wims was one of the few African American mail carriers in Montgomery County during this period, and delivered the mail in his two-horse team wagon on the Star Route between Clarksburg and Boyds. Delaware "Del" and Emily Wims lived here and then Melvin and Frances Wims lived here. The house which was next door has also been gone for many years, but the interior was photographed and shows the two different levels of the kitchen section and house. Purdums and Chaneys lived here over the years.

17. Day House

This two bay by two bay two-story house was built in 1925 for Clarence Denton and Dorothy Wilson Lawson Day. The style is American Foursquare wood frame with wrap-around porch. The porch roof is supported by tapered columns on brick piers with a balustrade. The facade has a dormer with a double window. The property was purchased from Thurston B. King. Some of the teachers at Clarksburg Grammar School boarded with the Days. In 1933 many motorists on Frederick Road were standed in a snow storm. The Days fed thirty-three people including Dr. and Mrs. Ruth Shaeffer. The property was sold to Duncan C. and Mabel E. Clark and it is now a nursery office.

18. site of Clarksburg Academy

Before the Clarksburg Grammar School was built, the Clarksburg Academy, a one-room school, was established in 1833. It was located behind the Day house on a parcel of "Money Worth" which was donated by William and Sarah Clarke Willson. The school's Trustees were: Horace Willson, Nacy Griffith, Elisha Lewis, Adamson Waters and James Hillard. They appointed teachers and assistants, and held the real estate. The teacher in 1860 was George Jackson, in 1869 the teacher was George W. Israel, who was followed by John S. Belt, who began in 1870, and then John Benson. Students were instructed in reading, writing, mathmatics, grammar and geography. In 1878 the school was turned over to the county. The building could accomodate up to 50 pupils. The county Trustees were: John Layton, James H. Miles, Charles Hill Murphy, and Obed Hurley. In the 1898 photograph below, the student fourth from the left in the back row was Selma Gibson. The teacher, Edith Byrne, resined in May of 1904. This building was converted to a residence and used until the early 1960's.

19. King Farm

This was the farm of John S. Belt and Laura P. Belt. They were married in 1867, and he was a school teacher at the Clarksburg Academy. Elias Vinson King purchased the property married Jemima Elizabeth Purdum and farmed here. Their house was built c. 1892 and had a five bay facade and shed roof porch. The interior brick chimneys provided heat for both floors. During World War II many articles were collected on the grounds and sold for scrap metal that were nearly one hundred years old; such as iron shackles and ball and chain sets. The tract was part of "Garnkirk" meaning church in the garden. The foundations of the barn and ice house exist today, but other outbuildings were the corncrib, tobacco barn, wagon shed and smoke house. The property was conveyed to Ora Henning King and his wife Iris Watkins King. Mr. King was a post master of Clarksburg. This was one of the first homes in the area to have a television set.

20. Larman Store

Cliff Larman operated a store, filling station and garage on Frederick Road. It was one of the few places in the area open on Sunday. In addition to selling fuel and repairing automobiles, Larman sold ice cream, candy and other delights.

21. Wims House and Sites of Interest

Clarksburg Methodist Episcopal Church picnic grounds were located across Frederick Road from Rocky Hill School. Several other homes were in this vicinity, including homes built by Wilson Wims. The house pictured below was built c. 1880's by Warner and Elizabeth Duffin Wims. Their daughter, Elsie Wims Carter, later lived here followed by Dorsey Disney, who purchased it c. 1985.

22. Watkins Store

The William Watkins Store was located just off Frederick Road, on what is now Running Brook Road. The Post Office was also located here at the time that this photograph was taken. The store was a one-and-a-half story frame building with a gable roof. The warehouse was located in the rear. The building was built on a fieldstone foundation, and the porch was added later, supported by square posts. After the Pleasant View Church was detroyed by fire in 1924, the congregation met in the store until the present John Wesley Methodist Church was built.

23. Watkins House

The house was built on a stone foundation c. 1880. The two-and-a-half story frame house stood next to the store. William Watkins lived here and ran the store c. 1890. In 1960 the left addition was constructed and in 1964 the house was sold to Charles R. and Jean Marks. After selling off several small parcels for houses, they sold the remaining property for development in 2000.

24. Benjamin "Bill" Wims House

This two-story four bay by one bay frame house with a gable roof was located on Old Baltimore Road. The Wims family has contributed to the history and growth of Clarksburg since the late 1860's. Many buildings such as the church, school and area homes were constructed by the descendants of the family pictured below.

25. John Wesley Methodist Church

The first church on this site was constructed in 1878 and was called Pleasant View and was part of the Boyd's Charge. Burials in the cemetery also date from that time. The first church burned in 1924 and the second church was built in the same location in 1925. The congregation met in the store across the road which was owned by Billy Watkins. The early Trustees included Warner Wims, Robert Gray, Thomas Jackson, William Davis, Perry Foreman, Arthur Gibbs, Lewis Riggs, and Maurice Mason. The name of the church was changed to John Wesley United Methodist in 1932. During the years that Reverend Harry J. McDonald was there the Women's Society of Christian Service was organized along with Methodist Youth Fellowship and the Epworth League. The Junior Choir was organized in 1953 and the choir loft was added in 1962. The pastors have been:

William P. Ryder 1886
J. W. Galloway
W. H. Brooks 1892
B. F. Myers 1889
Edward Moore 1889
Daniel Wheeler 1899
Bosley Boyce 1902
Nathan Ross 1906
J. S. Cole 1909

Rev. Lawson 1913
William Jefferson 1917
J. W. Langford 1919
W. P. Hopkins 1920
C. A. Randall 1921
J. H. Kent 1921
J. H. Lewis 1925
Melvin Johnson 1935
Robert Smith 1938
Harry J. McDonald 1939

C. E. O. Smallwood 1940
J. W. Langford 1953
Joseph Stemley 1959
Clifton Awkward 1962
R. Douglas Force 1968
Thomas W. Gregory 1971
Kenneth Jackson 1974
John Forkkio 1980
Dr. Haile

26. Rocky Hill School

Rocky Hill School was constructed in 1878 on one-quarter acre purchased for $50 from Abraham H. Rose. The community members built the school themselves and it was used until the enrollment was too low to warrant a community school. In 1884 the teacher was not paid due to lack of funds. The School Board appropriated $10 for an outhouse on February 8, 1887. In 1887 the School Board ordered that the pupils be combined with the Hyattstown School at Montgomery Chapel. The Rocky Hill School was constructed in the summer of 1894 insured for $400, and opened in September of that year. The one-room frame school housed 30 students in grades one through seven. Classes met in the Pleasant View Methodist Church until the building was ready. Students enjoyed playing dodge ball and baseball in the school yard and recall being called to class by the large bell in the gabled roof. Four rows of bench-style desks were bolted to the floor which featured desks hooked to the desk in front of the student. The younger students sat in the front, and lunch pails were left in a table with a lift top. At lunch time students ate around the two tables at the back of the room. At the front of the school was the teacher's desk, a bookcase for the 'library' and a blackboard. Students brought a cup from home to leave on their desk. The water was brought from the well at the Gibbs' home behind the school and left in a bucket. A wood burning stove furnished heat for the school. The older boys split wood and filled the wood box before school. Some afternoons after the floor was swept, the floor was disinfected with carbolic acid, and then oil was applied to keep the dust down. In 1901 the Washington and Gettysburg Railroad Company presented an application to the School Board asking for the right of way through the school lot. The proposal was referred to Ayton, King, and the Trustees, but the line never materialized. Students who wished continue their education could travel to Rockville. Those who did went on to become educators, professional people, and Roland Wims became a professor at Tuskegee Institute. Students walked to school until bus service was offered. Due to the bus fee, some families were unable to send all of their children on the bus. In 1932 a second room was added and a second teacher was hired. In 1952 the school was abandoned following the integration of the Montgomery County Schools. The old school was given to the John Wesley Church on September 9, 1952, but two years later the county bought it. In 1958 the M-NCPPC had the deed transferred, and later bought the property in 1961. The flagpole from the old school is still visible in front of the Senior Center. Some of the teachers were: Mr. Day, Lillian Giles, Miss Dorsey, Ella McNeal, Miss Datcher, Hannah B. Williams, Mrs. Otter, and Inez Hallman.

Roster of Students

Alma Day Alexander
Louise Green Alexander
Anna Moore Alexander

B. Lillian Bailey
Lucille Bailey
Matilda Bailey
Gertrude Wims Banks
Lorraine Naylor Bazilla
Anna Randolph Beckwith
Bertie Bell
Lena Green Blackman
Edward Boone
Leroy Bowie
Viola Foreman Brigham
Allan Glenwood Brown
Donald Brown
Evelyn Brown
James Brown
John Brown
Laura Brown
Louise Brown
Sam Brown
William Francis Brown
William Herbert Brown
William Joseph Brown
Alfred Brown
Eugene Byrd
Grant Byrd
Juanita Byrd
Roosevelt Byrd

Allen Cabell
Floyd Cabell
Phyliss Cabell
Raymond Cabell
Mary Turner Cabell
Gladys Carroll
Hazel Carroll
Helen Lyles Carroll
Lizzie Carroll
Virginia Moore Carter
James Chaney
John Henry Chaney
Louise Chaney
Phoebe Chaney
Alice Day Chase
Charlie Chase
Edward Chase
Etta Chase
Della Wims Chase
James Chase
John Chase
Joseph Chase
Louise Chase
William Chase
Urner Chase
Bernice Turner Clipper
Agnes Coates
William Coates
Ada Foreman Coleman
Marie Johnson Crocket
Rosie Wims Cuff
Patricia Curtis

Robert Davenport
Benjamin Davis
Dorothy Day
Irene Mason Day
Virgie Day
Juanita de Grafferied
Rita de Grafferied
Jerald Diggins
Thomas Dines
Dorothy Brown Disney
Cliffton Dorsey
George Dorsey
Irving Dorsey
Herman Dorsey
Lorraine Dorsey
William Dorsey
Ida May Doy
William Doy
Alice Duffin
Clara Foreman Duffin
Eleanor Duffin
Everline Duffin
Helen Duffin
Lorenza Duffin
Wallace Duffin
Alberta Dyson
Hazel Smallwood Dyson
Howell Dyson
Lillian Dyson
Melvin Dyson
Shirley Dyson

Lenora Foreman Edwards
Evelyn Fletcher
Bertha Moore Foreman
Clara Foreman
Ethel L. Foreman
Frances Wims Foreman
Francis C. Foreman
Frederick Foreman
Hattie Foreman
Helen E. Foreman
John Henry Foreman
Joseph Foreman
Leslie Perry Foreman
Lorraine Jackson Foreman
Rebecca Foreman
Robert Leroy Foreman
Roland Alfonzo Foreman
T. Arthur Foreman
Thomas Foreman
William Foreman
William A. Foreman
William H. Foreman
Zelma L. Foreman

Delores Hackey Gamble
Alfred Genus
Charles Genus
Eugene Genus
Hartley Genus
Henry Genus
Leo Genus
Lillian Genus
Anna Gibbs
Edna Gibbs
Mary Gibbs

Roster of Students

Raymond Gibbs
Virgie Gibbs
Betty Gibbs
Catherine Gray
Doris Gray
Edna Gray
Eula Gray
Elizabeth Gray
Frances Gray
Ianthia Gray
Irene Gray
Jean Gray
John Henry Gray
Jessie Gray
Margaret Gray
Mabel Louise Gray
Mary Catherine Gray
Matilda Mason Gray
Oliver Gray
Shirley Gray
Thelma Gray
Auther Green
Carroll Green
Earl Green
James Green
John Willis Green
Hattie Foreman Green

Artie Snowden Hackey
Dorothy Hackey
Douglas Hackey
Ernest Hackey
Fay Foreman Hackey
George Hackey
Harvey Hackey, Jr.
James Hackey
John Hackey
Leroy Hackey
Virginia Hackey
Mildred Hackey
Constance Randolph Hall
Edward Hall
Manard Hall
Minnie Hall

William Hammond
Rita Harris
Robert Harris
Christine Hawkins
Howard Hawkins
James Hawkins
Marie Jackson Hawkins
Ellis Hebron
Louise Coates Hebron
David Holland
Eugene Holland
Dunbar Honemond
Otis Hope

Ashton Jackson
Bernadine Jackson
Edward Jackson
Elwood Jackson
Lewellyn Jackson
Melvin Jackson
Nathan Jackson
Nettie Jackson
Loraine Jackson
Sylvester Jackson
Thomas Jackson
Upton Jackson
Guy Johnson
Hayes Johnson
Helen Johnson
Marie Johnson
Melvin Johnson
Pat Johnson
Paul Johnson
Rex Johnson
Mary Day Johnson
Preston Johnson
Robert Johnson
Patricia Curtis Johnson
Vivian Johnson
Evelyn Jolly
Clifton Jones

Pauline Kinard
William Kinard

Willy Lee
Alice Foreman Lincoln
Jacqueline Lowery
Forrest Lyles
Helena Genus Lyles
Joseph Lyles
Josephine Foreman Lyles
Theodore Lyles
William Marshall Lyles

Eugene Martin
Jerry Martin
Howard Mason
James Mason
James S. Mason
John Mason
Sherman Mason
Stanley Mason
Alfred Moore
Charley Moore
Della Moore
George Walter Moore
Georgia Moore
Lawrence Moore
May Moore
Samuel Moore
Stanley Moore

Arthur Naylor
Eleanor Naylor
Gladys Naylor
Helen Naylor
Kenneth Naylor
Mae Wims Naylor
Mary Roby Naylor
Pauline Naylor
Richard Naylor
Sarah Wims Neal
Donald Noland

Pearl Luckett Owens

Charley Pendelton
Leona Pendelton

Roster of Students

Madeline Perry
Florence Turner Phillips
Ellen Plummer
Estelle Randolph Plummer
Henry Plummer
Lottie Plummer
Thomas Plummer
Virginia Sims Plummer
Agnes Moore Posey
Jospeh Powell
Mabel Mason Prather
Lillie Suggs Proctor
Proctor Family

Macadoo Ramey
Thelma Ramey
Arthur Randolph
Bobby Randolph
Carlton Randolph
Donald Randolph
Ellen Randolph
Garnett Randolph
Howard Randloph

Kenneth Randolph
Maggie Chase Randolph
Park Randolph
Viola Randolph
Walter Randolph
Bernetta Hawkins Ricks
David Robinson
Delores Robinson
Helen Robinson
Joseph Robinson
Sadie Ross

MacArthur Turner
Sadie Turner
Susie Turner
Minnie Turner Tyler

Charles Washington
Gladys Carroll Washington
Annie Day Weedon
Grace Jackson Williams
Elizabeth Foreman Williams
Margaret Foreman Williams

Althea Wims
Beatrice Wims
Benjamin Wims
Daniel Wims
Granison Wims
Herbert Wims
Leonard Wims
Maude Wims
Mary Wims
Maynard Wims
Melvin Wims
Rena Wims
Roland Wims
Rosa Wims
Russell Wims
Wallace Wims

Gertrude Young

John Young

This roster of students does not reflect the total school enrollment

Students of Rocky Hill School

Front Row Left to Right: Phoebe A. Dorsey, Helena Lyles, Mary Jackson, James Hackey, Charles Johnson, Charles Moore, ?, Battle Lou Chase, ?, George Greene, James Brown, Samuel Foreman, Henry Chaney.
Second Row: James E. Chaney, Thomas Chase, Mary Catherine Gray, George Hackey, Ella Brown, Estelle Randolph, Nell Foreman, Lenora Foreman, Elizabeth Randolph, ?.
Third Row: William Foreman, John Hackey, Clinton Imes, Alice Day.
Fourth Row: Alberta Dyson, Lillian Bailey, Beulah Johnson, Lena Greene, Anna Randolph, Matilda Bailey, Louise Brown, Matilda Gray, Lucille Gray.
Back Row: Herbert Brown, Lillian Dyson, Walter Randolph, Virginia Gray, Oscar Hackey, James Greene, Lawrence Moore, Inez Hallman and Emanuel Snowden.

Students of Rocky Hill School

Front Row Left to Right: ?, ?, ?, ?, William Talley, ?, Leroy Hackett, Sadie Turner, Rosa Wims, Guy Johnson, Louise Alexander, Joe Power, Constance Hall, ?, ?, William Hall. Middle: Evelyn Brown, Gladys Naylor, Annie Catherine Day, Margaret Williams, ?, ?, ?, ?, Lottie Plummer, ?, Bertie Bell Foreman, Betty Hawkins, Edith Mallory, Agnes Coates, Faye Hackey, Virginia Sims, ?, Douglas Hackey, Irvin Dorsey, ?, ?.

27. Dowden's Ordinary

The structure pictured below was built in 1753 and opened for business in July of 1754. The log building was L shaped and featured a shingled roof with multiple dormers. That year Michael Ashford Dowden applied for a permit to operate a public house of entertainment. Stage coaches stopped here twice weekly, private carriages and travelers on horseback came frequently. They shared news and quenched their thirst before resuming their journey. From April 15-17, 1755 General Edward Braddock and his troops camped here on their way to Frederick. Braddock made the tavern his headquarters. A snow storm blew many of their tents down, but the soldiers would face worse matters at Fort Duquesne. In 1765 Michael Dowden was required by the British to purchase stamps for paperwork when he posted bail for James Veatch. Clarksburg, still part of Frederick County, saw the twelve Frederick County Justices meet at the tavern that November to formally object to the "stamp." They came to an agreement that the English Parliament could not decide who and when to tax without the local government's input. Furthermore, they objected to the Colonist's bearing the cost of the standing British Army. The resulting court action is now known as the Repudiation Act of 1765. The Sons of Liberty made the tavern their meeting place, too. They were formed to support the action of the court and Lower House of the Maryland Assembly. Members of the Sons of Liberty Societies included the Bealls, Belts, Clarkes, Dowdens, Williams, Willsons, and Waters.

John Dowden continued operating the establishment after his father's death in the 1780's. The tavern was sold to Basil Roberts who added horse racing, a ladies sitting room and changed the name of the establishment to Robert's Tavern. Frederick Scholl was the subsequent owner, who passed the tavern to his son Jacob Scholl. It was he who planted the clippings given to him by a guest and subsequently served Catawba wine here. Leonard Dent Shaw purchased the tavern and it was he who loaned his name to area, which is known as Shaw Hill. He added a blacksmith shop and converted the hotel rooms into apartments which he rented to local farm workers. James Titus Bennett and two of his sons lived here c. 1906 and later Jack Mason, Will Brown and his family were among the last one's to live on the premises.

On April 1915 two thousand gathered to see the Janet Montgomery Chapter of the D. A. R. unveil the memorial on the site of Dowden's Ordinary. Mrs. Stone presented a speech outlining the events which had occured at the tavern over the years. Then Olivia and Robert Green, descendants of Michael Dowden, unveiled the plaque while the Engineer's Band played the "Star Spangled Banner." Following the bendiction members of the D. A. R. gathered on the platform and sang "My Country Tis of Thee." At the time of the unveiling only the tavern portion of the once large building was still standing. The section that had been a seventeen room hotel had already been torn down. The tavern was decorated in flags for the ceremony. The British flag was on display courtesy of the British Ambassdor Sir Cecil Spring Rice. The 1910 census lists Asa Hyatt Welsh here as a whiskey distiller and grocer, renting the place. The remaining part of Dowden's Ordinary was torn down c. 1924 due to it's delapidated condition. The land was sold to Edward Deets and then to Gary and Merry Ellen Poole. The Clarksburg by-pass will pass with 150 feet of this historic site, but the Maryland National Capitol Park and Planning Commission plans to purchase the land where the building sat and boulder remains.

28. Hammer Hill

This land was patented to Michael A. Dowden on November 10, 1752. The 40 acres are situated on the east end of Clarksburg near Wafford's Branch which flows into the Little Seneca Creek. The property was owned by Jacob Scholl who propagated Catawba Grapes here. Frederick Scholl was operating the tavern by 1800. Jeremiah Orme, a grocer in Georgetown, D. C., sold wine made from the Catawba grape in the 1820's. According to Scholl's son Mountjoy, who was born in 1792, the plants were given to his father when Mountjoy was a youngster. The guest gave him two cuttings, and the vineyard in Clarksburg resulted. Plants were then cultivated in Rockville, then in Cincinnati, Ohio and later in St. Louis. Scientists came to Clarksburg to study the grape. The Honorable George W. Hilton purchased the property which is on the tract called "Hammer Hill". After he built a house in Clarksburg, the farm was managed by Leonard Dent Shaw, blacksmith. Farm laborers in 1880 included John Snowden, John Porter, William Porter, and John Wims. The property was purchased from the Lewis family in 1891 by Dr. James Edward and Sarah Isabella Henderson Deets who had the present Queen Anne style three-story house completed by 1899. Dr. Deets completed his medical training at the University of Maryland and chose to live near his wife's family in Montgomery County. The architecture of "Hammer Hill" is different than the other houses in Clarksburg and exudes the fashionable details of the period. The porch is ornately trimmed with turned posts, jig-saw bric-a-brac and the double paneled doors have transoms and side lights. The side porch has a conservatory. Dr. Deets deeded it to Edward H. Deets and in 1963 his wife Nelle sold it to the Atherly family. Robert and Edith Hoffman purchased the property from James Moore and sold it to Gary and Merry Ellen Poole who live here presently. The Clarksburg bypass will pass within 150 feet of the historic house.

29. Hilton House

This house was located next to Hammer Hill and was the home of Charles Scott Hilton and family. Pictured in the photograph are Gladys Neale Hilton, Anna Mary Tyrell Hilton and Charles S. Hilton. The house was built c. 1850 and was white clapboard with green shutters. It had a rear ell, three bedrooms, center hall, Latrobe stove, a large dining room and kitchen. The ice box was on the back porch. On the adjoining lot was another home which is no longer standing, that of Dr. Thomas K. Galloway. Author Thomas H. Stocton Boyd lived in this house with his mother, Elizabeth, in 1880. Elizabeth was the widow of Rev. Reuben T. Boyd. T. H. S. Boyd was a journalist who in 1879 published "The History of Montgomery County, Maryland, From It's Earliest Settlement in 1650 to 1879." A later inventory of Clarksburg lists this house as the bungalow of William K. and B. L. Watkins. The lot was owned by Rodney H. and A. T. Darby in the late 1970's. The present house on this property was built by Henry E. "Shook" King who was a local huckster. His widow Edna May Norwood King raised their children here. The Green Ridge Baptist Church rented the house for $100 a month from 1970-1972 before building their church.

30. Murphy House

In 1880 Charles Hill Murphy's widow Mary Richardson Murphy was living here with her daughters. She was his second wife, and a sister to his first wife, Julia Ann Richardson Murphy. The family was active in the Methodist church, civic affairs, the Clarksburg Literary Association and state government. The house is visible on the left side of the photograph, south of Hilton's store. The sign on the store reads "Celluloid Starch".

31. Hilton's Store

Charles S. Hilton was a son of George Washington Hilton and Frances Columbia Scott Hilton. Both men were postmasters of Clarksburg. The frame two-story store was built prior to 1857, when the post office was there for several years. The front gable roof has returned cornices and a circular window in the gable. The half round window on the facade have curved shutters, giving an interesting pattern to the second story. The three bay first floor has a center door flanked by two windows. The sign on the side reads "celluloid starch". The sign over the door reads "Clarksburg Post Office" dating the photograph to the period when the post office was located here again from 1901 until 1911. The emblem on the post indicates that telegrams could be received and sent from this location.

32. Miles House

The original structure may have been built for John Belt prior to 1783. It was later the home of George Washington Hilton and his wife Frances Columbia Scott Hilton. George died in 1892 and Robert S. and Sarah Catherine Miles Hilton lived here until 1911. John and Laura Estelle Price Gardner purchased the property in 1911 and had the cabin torn down to make room for their new house. The two-story frame house with Victorian influences has twelve rooms and has a wrap around porch. A. Philip Brodsky purchased the property and then in July of 1980 Dee M. and Dorothy L. Wilson purchased the home which now houses a Bridal Shop and Antiques. The side facing gables have widows, as does the facade, and the porch supports have decorative cornice work. The balustrade extends the length of the front porch.

33. Clarksburg School

Land for the Clarksburg School was deeded from Dr. James E. Deets and Sarah C. Hilton. The school opened on November 4, 1909. The frame building was originally a two-room school with a vestibule and cloakroom. The facade is decorated with fish scale shingles in the gable and returned cornices. The windows are four over four paned rectangular, and balance the door and transom symetrically. Some of the teachers over the years were Mary Lowe Smith, Elmyra Parrish, Mary Morningstar, Lenore Hersman Marks, Alice Leighton Schmidt, Anna Austin Roberts, Viola Bleckley, Libby Welde, and Mrs. Gouth. During the rest period after recess Mary Lowe Smith played music which enriched her pupils lives. In the 1930's the classrooms were painted brown and a blackborad covered one wall. For many years Del Wims was the janitor here. Alice Leighton Schmidt taught from 1943 - 1954 and saw many changes during those years. A frame addition was built in 1942, and brick additions were constructed in the 1950's and 1960's. In 1944 a request was submitted for sanitary facilities and heat. The building then served as the Head Start facility and the principal was Marie Griffin. The building was moved 400 feet in 1973 to make way for the library addition to the new school. The building is currently used for arts and crafts classes. In 1975 the old school was added to the National Register of Historic Places. Students not pictured who attended here include: Howard M. Miles, Henry Miles, Thomas Day, Louisa Lewis, Margaret Lewis, Gloria King, Eloise Haney, Ora Henning King, Barbara Cordell, Janet Cordell, Kitty Beck, Tommy Johnson, Douglas Swank, Helen Cole, Perry Andrews, Otis Norwood, Carol Thompson, Bonnie Whipp, Shirley Jewell, Winston Burdette, Louise Hough, Francis Dallor and Donald Burdette.

Holding banner: Earl Richards, Dora Thompson, Charles Dronenburg. Row 1: Julian Nichols, Edward Miles, Laura Virginia Miles, Helen Richards, Leo Jamison, Edward Cordell, Marie Chick, Dorothy Fay Righter, Miller Day, James Cordell, Stephen Nelson. Row 2: Elizabeth Miles, Grace Thompson, Bob Dronenburg, Mary Katherine Miles, Marguerite Barr, Paul Nelson, Kenneth Price, Joyce Day, Mary Lowe Smith, Teacher. Row 3: Wordna Edwards, Lorraine Dronenburg, Pete King, Sarah Titus, Lindon Stottlemyer, Frances Rubel, and Hubert Nichols.

First Grade Class, back row second from right is Oliver King c. 1947

An interior photograph of Clarksburg School gives one a glimpse into a bygone era. Heated by the pot-bellied, coal-burning, stove in the middle of the classroom, cooled by open windows, students learned their lessons in rows of desks. The janitor got the fire started in the mornings, but the teacher was responsible for keeping the fire going on cold days. The upright piano provided accompaniment for their songs, and President Washington's picture hangs near the progress chart on an otherwise bare wall. Not shown was the aquarium which had gold fish. Eloise Haney Woodfield recalls a field trip to the woods across the road, and going down behind the school to get water for the gold fish.

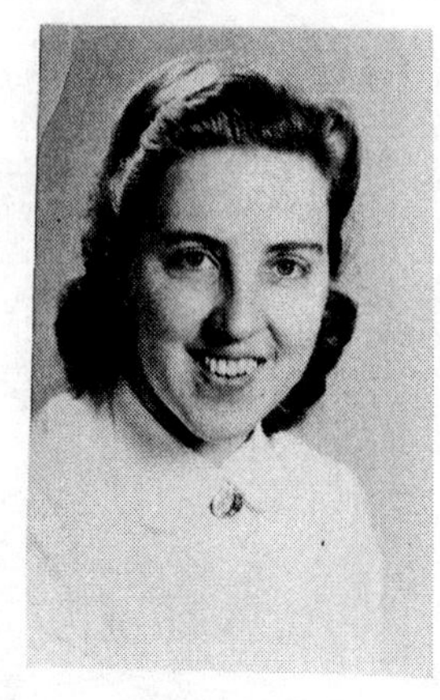

Teachers: Anna Austin, Alice Leighton, Libby Welde, Lenore Hersman

Del Wims

Teachers Alice Leighton Schmidt, Mary Morningstar and Viola Bleckley

34. Moneysworth Farm

Pictured is the rear section of this home which was a one-story log house constructed of chestnut logs c. 1760. When the front section was built c. 1860 most of the original home was adapted into the new house. The Redgrave Family moved from England in 1948 and farmed here. The farm property was divided by I-270 in the 1960's and then a portion of the property was used for the Kingsley Wilderness School. Presently the log house is being renovated and will be used by Kingsley for programs after the adjoining correctional facility is completed.

35. Leonidas Willson House

This lot was acquired from Benjamin Browning in 1816 and, at that time, was denoted as lot 4, with a dwelling on it. The frame section of this house was built for William and Sarah Jupine Clarke Willson c. 1840. Several log outbuildings remain from this period. William purchased the house and trading post from his father-in-law. Willam's parents were Elizabeth Perry Scholl Willson and John Willson of Jonathan. It was during this period that the front frame section was constructed. The center hall has two rooms on each side with plaster medallions in the ceiling. From these are suspended crystal chandeliers. The living room has a painted marbelized sandstone fireplace. William's son, Leonidas and Maria Willson, purchased his sibling's share of their inheritance in 1869 and became the owner of the house. Leonidas was a graduate of Yale University in the 1830's who returned to Clarksburg to become the co-proprietor of the store. After Maria E. Harris Willson's death the house was sold in 1911 to Charles and Mary Waters. The two-and-a-half story white frame house with full-length front porch has beautiful supports adorning the posts. The double front door features a three-light transom and two-light sidelights. The house is three bay by two bay and was built on a fieldstone foundation. There are three interior chimneys. Howard and Ardella Mae King Miles purchased the house in 1917 and as automobile owners took to the road Clarksburg saw a slight resurgence in the tourist trade. The Italianate details were added after the house became known as "The Boxwood Inn," the boarding house run by the Miles. In 1962 Dr. Howard C. and W. J. Graves purchased the house and undertook it's renovation.

36. Clarke-Waters-Sellman House

The 1797 log section of this house was built on lot 5 for John Buxton and sold to John G. Clarke, Jr., the founder of Clarksburg and his wife Ann Archey Clarke. The house was conveyed to their daughter Sarah Jupine Clarke and her husband William Willson in 1803. The will states that William was the executor and that the couple had been living here prior to 1802 when the will was written. The front section is a five bay by two bay, two-and-a-half story frame house built on a fieldstone foundation. This section was built between 1840 and 1845. There are two interior chimneys and one exteroir fieldstone chimney. From 1865-1870 Baker T. Silance rented the house and operated his shoemaking in a small building next to the house. The house remained in the Willson family as their daughter Mary Willson Neel Waters conveyed it to her daughter Sarah Isabel Neel Sellman. Sarah married Alonzo Sellman, and their son William A. Sellman was the last of the family to live here. Sarah also took in boarders such as the teacher William H. Pace, his wife, and daughter; and Henson Buxton who clerked in Gibson's Store. George and Mary Louisa Hughes lived here before the house was sold in 1923 to Margaret Halvosa. Catherine Beck lived here with Mrs. Halvosa who sold it to Georgie Carmine Dudrow Darby in 1937. During the remodeling papers from the 1790's were found in the walls. John D. Heckert purchased the house in 1973.

37. Site of Poole Cabin

This was lot 6 and the log cabin was the home of W. and Josephine Hurley Humrichouse in 1856. The cabin was then the home of Clarence Robert and Lillie Mae Beall Poole, but was later abandoned. During this time neighborhood boys enjoyed using the structure as a fort. Eventually the home was torn down to make make way for the stucco house built for Ralph Fraley and Barbara Martz. Below is the view from across the street where the cabin stood looking toward Hyattstown.

38. Power House

The original rear one-story log section was built for John Nelson Burnside on lot 9 c. 1820 who operated an old tan-yard between here and the site of Lewis home. The log house was purchased by John Poole in 1823, who sold it to Isaac N. and Elizabeth Power in 1831. The property was assessed at $144 in 1838 but for $500 in 1841, after the front two-and-a-half story section was added c. 1840. This section was built on a stone foundation and was five bay by three bay. Mary L. Power was Clarksburg's Post Master from 1865 until 1873 while this post office was a distribution point for the communities of Boyds, Hyattstown, King's Valley, Purdum, Browningsville, Comus, and Lewisdale. The clapboard siding was covered in asbestos siding about this time. Kate Purdum purchased the house from the heirs of Mary L. Power and lived here from 1926 until 1951. The house was later sold to Robert L. and R. J. Whalen.

39. Winemiller-Gibson House

This two-and-a-half story frame Tidewater house was built on lot 9 c. 1840 for John Winemiller, Jr. after he purchased the tannery property which adjoined this land on the north. The house had clapboard siding, arched windows, three chimneys, and a two-story rear porch. The front porch roof was supported by posts with decorative dental cornice work. The property was sold at public auction to Rufus Magruder in 1849. He was the last tanner to operate Clarksburg's largest employer. When the property sold to John H. Gibson in 1857 the tannery operation closed. Gibson and his partner Thomas Nicholls had a store built on the adjoining parcel, and the Gibson family lived here until Charles Gibson sold it to William H. Leaman, rural mail carrier, in 1922. The house was sold to James I. Mullen in 1971 and was left vacant and boarded up. When Jim Mullen wanted to have a septic holding tank built and the county restricted him from doing this, he obtained a demolition permit. The historic house with the beautiful architectural detail was demolished.

40. Power's Farm

Where the I-270 cloverleaf is presently, once stood the Power's farm. Isaac Power owned this land and farmed here, but by 1879, the property belonged to Elizabeth Powers. The two-story frame house had a five bay facade with a central doorway. The second story bay was semi-octagonal, with a dormer in the in the slope of the roof. The shed-roofed porch had four octagonal doric columns. There were two internal brick end chimneys and the gables had returned cornice. The house was standing until 1976.

41. Hotel-Lewis House

Built c. 1860 the hotel was owned by Hilton and Kemp and operated by Julia Cummings. The bar tender in 1860 was John Boyer, perhaps he served whiskey made at the nearby King's Distillery. In 1878 John Baker was the hotel operator and subsequently Richard Thompson in 1883. His wife, six children, and mother-in-law lived here also. James H. Kemp lived here in 1880. In 1903 the property was owned by Martha J. Kemp when Frances Columbia Scott Hilton defaulted on the payments. A Trustee's Sale was held on July 11, 1903 in front of the Hotel and the advertisement described the building as 12 rooms with closets, 2 attic rooms, a two-story rear addition with 4 rooms, a cellar, and 2 porches. The two acre lot included a carriage shed, livery stable smoke house, poultry house, large back yard, a never failing pump of water, and a fine garden. The ad also states that the property adjoined the lots of Charles William Gibson, the late John H. Gibson, and the farm of the late Leonidas Willson. The property sold for $900 and was listed as one of the oldest hostelries in the county. The 1910 census has William Edward Lewis, transit trade and boarding house. This house was later conveyed to his son John Edward Lewis. They took in boarders, and his mother lived in the rear ell. The original windows were poured glass and the hand hewn logs supported the house over the basement. During the 1970's the owner obtained a liquor liscense using the residence as a tavern. Jim Grey was the last occupant before the building was torn down to make way for a bank. There were four springs on the property and during the construction of Rt. 121 the waters from the springs had to be diverted under the road to Ten Mile Branch. During the process wooden vats were uncovered that had been used in the 1880's.

42. Store and warehouse

This was lot 10 and formerly the Burnside tannery property. John Nelson Burnside fell heir to two lots following the death of his father Joseph in 1816. John moved the family business to this site and was the foreman of the tannery which was established by 1820. He married Nancy Talbot and lived in Clarksburg until she died. The tannery was sold to Robert Beam in 1831, then to John Winemiller, Jr. in 1838, who had the adjoining house built. In 1849 Rufus Magruder purchased the tannery and sold it in 1857 to Thomas Nicholls and John Gibson. They opened a store c. 1860 on the tannery property. Advertisements for the Gibson Store exist as far back as 1878 when an advertisement for the store reads: J. H. Gibson, dealer in Dry Goods and Groceries, Hardware, Boots, Shoes, Hats, Drugs and Medicines, Notions, etc. The warehouse was located directly behind the store. In 1895 this store was replaced with a larger two story building pictured below. This store was operated by Levi Price, who moved here from Hyattstown. The hall over the store was used as the Community Hall. Locals put on amateur plays and musical entertainments. The store was also the polling place for many years and the Post Office was located until William Dronenburg purchased the store and lived in one section of the building. The old store later became the Hillside Apartment Building, owned by Fred Cushman. The store was demolished in the 1950's.

43. site of Doctor's Office and Anderson House

The first of these three lots was the location of Dr. Rezin R. Thompson's office in 1865, and later Dr. E. C. Worthington. It was later listed as the property of William Earl and E. L. Thompson. The adjacent lot was owned by Thomas S. Nichols in 1865 and had a log house on it. The third of the lots was the the site of the Charles Thomas Anderson house and shop built c. 1869. C. T. Anderson was a successful carriage maker and wheel wright. He also patented several inventions. His wife was Eliza Ann Hurley Anderson. Their daughter Altie married William W. Dronenburg who lived here for a few years. Then Lon Anderson lived here in the 1920's. Anderson was a mechanic who worked on Model A and T Fords.

44. Burner House

In 1879 this was the site of Howard Young's house. Paul and Neva Thompson Burner had the present house built in the early 1930's. The bungalow style house is one-and-a-half stories with a center dormer. The three-bay frame house was later sold when the Burner's built the brick house further up the road. The Burner's also ran a garage here and Jim Burner later lived in the shop building near the garage.

45. Leaman - Cordell House

In 1865 this was the site of Obed Hurley's house. In 1879 Richard and John F. Leaman were living on adjoining property here. Richard Leaman was a blacksmith and John was an agent for an organ company which had salesmen take a sample organ around to take orders in homes. The two-story frame house is three bay by one bay with a gable roof and decorative work in the eaves. The porch has a shed roof supported by square posts and a balustrade. In later years Eugene and Nettie J. Cordell lived here. Ed Cordell had the smaller house built in 1946 on a parcel. There was a road leading to the mill called Bone Mill Road off Frederick Road. The mill produced fertilizer from animal bones. A wagon went to local farms to pick up dead animals which were brought here. For a horse, the famer was given a box of soap. Marshall Day recalled that members of his family worked here.

46. Stephen Lewis House

Inside this frame house are two log cabins joined by a central stairway. Stephen Lewis purchased lots 10, 11, and 12 between 1797 and 1831 in Clarksburg on the tract "Moneyworth." The cabins may have already been there. There were also stables, a blacksmith shop and other outbuildings when Camden R. Nicholls purchased the property following Stephen Lewis' death in 1853. Nicholls deeded the property to Sarah and Thomas Nichols, his daughter and son-in-law. It was farmed by Edward King Lewis and subsequently, his son John A. Lewis. James E. Williams purchased the farm from Nichols in 1878, about the same time that the cabins were incorporated into a frame house. The addition on the south end is a one-story wing, as is the kitchen addition on the north end. Williams sold the farm in 1905 to Mahlon T. Lewis, son of Edward King and Mary Ann T. King Lewis. The Larmans owned the farm before Doody Burkett purchased it in 1936. In 1954 the property was divided by the construction of Interstate 270. The present owners plan to operate a catering company from the house.

47. Snow Hill

Basil Soper operated the Snow Hill Ordinary from 1783 until the house burned. The house was a two-story five bay by one bay frame structure with a gable roof. The center gable facade had a widow and ginger bread bric-a-brac. The full-length front porch had a shed roof covered with raised seam metal and was supported by seven turned, bracketed posts. The house was heated by two double brick chimneys. The American four-square which was subsequently built on the site was called Angel Hill. John Studderford lived here, followed by Robert Byrd. The next house was Ab and Bertha Chick's two-story frame farmhouse. Known as Chick's Corner, the farm was bisected when I-270 was constructed. The stave mill was located next after the house on this site was torn down. Down the lane between these two farms was the Jamison farm, and down Comus Road was the Whipp store and residence.

48. Brashears House

This land was previously part of a farm on which the log house of Edwin N. Darby was built c. 1836. Darby married Sarah Ann Holland and raised nine children and farmed here. In the 1940's Marjorie Brashears lived in the present house with her daughters, followed by the Frys. Also, Mary Ellen and Bill Simpson lived here briefly.

49. Burdette House

Formerly this land was part of the Darby farm. Later Newman Dudrow purchased this property, including the frame tenant house close to the road which burned down. Harry and Margaret Burdette lived in the brick Colonial Revival style house. There are six bedrooms upstairs, three on each side of the long hall.

50. Sunnyside Restaurant

William Wilson Cecil and his wife Maggie Kinna Cecil opened a filling station on 355 at the intersection with their farm lane. They had a small bedroom in the back, and sold produce from the farm. Maggie expanded the enterprise by cooking soup and fixing sandwiches. She had her regular customers and knew what each preferred. In the photograph, notice the old gasoline pump's hose which drained the fuel from the top tank, prior to electric pumps.

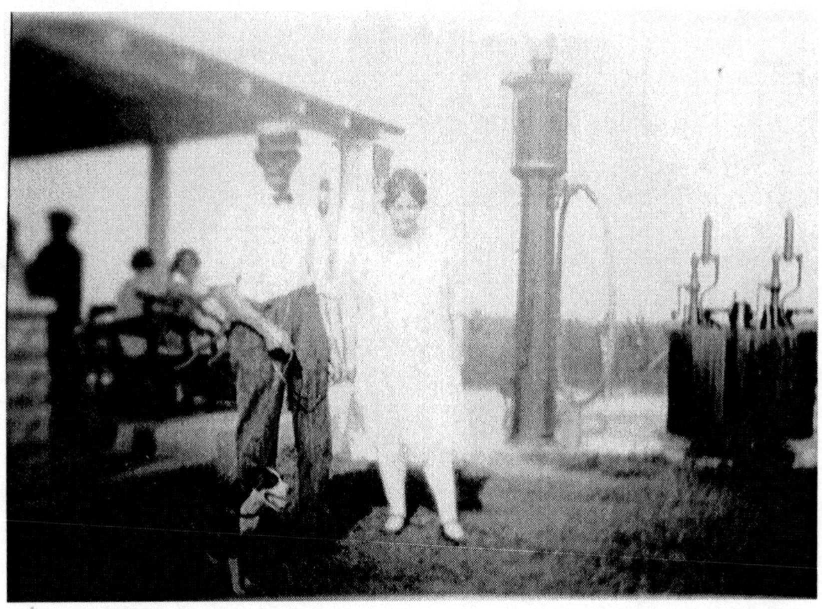

51. Silver Hill Farm

One of the early Murphy farms was run by George Washington Murphy and sold to Ed Miles and William Wilson Cecil in the 1920's. When the interstate was constructed most of the farm land was used for the north bound lanes of 270. Mrs. Reed was the last owner of the property. This house, which had three bedrooms, a parlor, kitchen and dining room is no longer standing. It was a two-story four bay by two bay frame house with brick end chimneys. The full-length front porch had a shed roof and was supported by square posts on piers. The outbuildings included a turkey pen and house, bank barn, smoke house, barrack for the hay, pigpen, spring house, corn crib, and a garage. In August of 1925 William and Maggie Kinna Cecil celebrated their wedding anniversary by holding a family reunion on the farm. The families of his eleven brothers and sisters arrived in ten model-T Fords. This photograph was taken at that occasion.

52. Cordell House

This was the home of Russell Cordell, Welty Cordell and Mamie Cordell. They were all children of John Henry and Mary Ellen Cordell. It is a one-story three bay by two bay bungalow. The dormer has a double window and the porch roof is supported by four posts. The house is beside the Clarksburg Methodist Church on Spire Street and was built c. 1938. Michael Siers and Janet Cordell Siers live here presently.

53. Methodist Episcopal Church

Methodists officially formed the Clarksburg Congregation on June 5, 1788. The group was part of the Montgomery Circuit which included the oldest Methodist congregation at Sugarloaf [Comus] and Goshen. After meeting in members' homes, some of the meetings were held at the Methodist Camp Meeting grounds. Property for the first Meeting House was acquired from John Clarke on October 24, 1794 on three-quarters of an acre parceled from the tract "Warfield's Vineyard." The Trustees were John Clarke, Samuel Hobbs, Basil Soper, Archibald Browning, Jonathan Browning, Jr., Joseph Waters, and Archibald Hawkins. The log church was called Ebenezer Chapel and was austere and plain. The benches were planks with no backs, the floor was wooden planks, and the pulpit was three feet from the floor in a tall narrow box shape. Weekly expenses included candles and chopping wood. The average weekly collection was thirty-three cents, with an average annual collection being $5.45. In 1853 the old chapel was replaced by a brick church. It was two stories high with a balcony for the black members. In 1857 additional land was purchased for the adjoining cemetery. In 1865 the denomination split and some members left to form the Methodist Episcopal South. In 1904 a fence was constructed around the cemetery. The posts for the entrance are still standing. The lumber was furnished by Randolph H. Windsor. The church lot was also fenced and hitching lines were added at a cost of $267.89. A lawn fete and oyster supper raised the money to fund the project. The fence was painted for $27.85.

The present Clarksburg Methodist Church was built in 1909 by Webster Vorhees Burdette. The lumber was furnished by Robert S. Hilton at $7.00 per 1000 feet. The cornerstone was laid during an evening ceremony held on September 15, 1909. Mr. Sumwalt spoke and then Mrs. Cornelia Elizabeth Shriner Benson sang "The Holy City." It was dedicated on December 17, 1909 by Bishop Cranston. The Trustees at that time were: James Hening Purdum, John W. Byrne, William R. Windsor, James E. King, John W. Ashton, James Franklin Purdum, and John S. Buxton. The brick church was demolished and the windows were sold. In 1923 the wooden steps were replaced by concrete steps. The two denominations were reunited in 1939 and on November 10, 1940 the Clarksburg United Methodist Church was formed.

The Pastors of the Montgomery Circuit were:

Robert Green & John Allen 1788
James Wilson & John Childs 1789
George Haggerty & John Roagan 1790
John Rowan & Aquilla Garrettson 1791
Joshua Wells & Thomas Bell 1792
Morris Howe & Regin Simpson 1793
Freeborn Garrettson & Th. Wayman 1794
Beverly Waugh 1815
C. Fry & W. L. Gibson 1824
Caleb Reynolds & J. G. Watt 1827
Basil Berry & James Reed, Sr. 1828
Philip D. Lipscomb & D. Miller 1834
Jacob Larkin & E. Miller 1835
James Reiley & J. Young 1837
Richard Brown & J. W. Cronin 1838
Isaac Collins & J. H. Brown 1841
J. M. Jones & R. H. W. Brent 1842
John Hurst & Basil Berry 1843
Horace Holland & Joseph Phelps 1844
Horace Holland & John W. Stark 1845
H. W. Enos & J. S. Grosuch 1846
H. W. Enos & William G. Cross 1847
William Hank & William Chapman 1848
James Munroe & Chas. G. Linthicum 1849
Geo. W. Israel & Sam'l Cornelius 1850
George W. Israel & M. L. Pugh 1851
J. W. Collin & Henry Seever 1852
J. M. Grandin & P. B. Brown 1854
Charles A. Reed & L. D. Hennon 1856
Charles A. Reed & G. R. Jefferson 1857
Samuel Cornelius & Wm. Magruder 1858
John L. Gilbert & Sam'l Cummings 1860
Samuel V. Leech & C. H. Mytinger 1862
William Holliday & E. E. Shipley 1864
J. W. Start & E. E. Shipley 1866
J. W. Start & G. W. Hobbs 1867
James D. Still & D. M. Browning 1869
Harrison McNemar & J. S. M. Haslip 1871
T. Marshall West 1874
Emory Burhman 1877
Randolph Richardson Murphy 1880
W. R. Gwinn & A. H. Thompson 1883
Thomas J. Cross & A. H. Thompson 1886
J. R. Pardew 1890
W. F. Roberts 1892
J. W. Steele 1894
William H. Harris 1896
Elmer Eugene Marshall 1899
Caleb M. Yost 1902
Thomas S. Davis 1911
Walter S. Jones 1917
Frank Y. Jaggers 1920
Wallace M. Brashears 1923
Fred R. Barnes 1926
Hartwell Fitch Chandler 1935
Thomas Morgan 1939
Herbert Clyde Chaffer 1946
Jack G. Ammon 1948
Ben F. Hartley 1954
Howard Allwine 1959

Lorne Burton 1960
Lloyd McClarren 1970
Kenneth Beall 1973
J. Howard Link 1976
Edgar Moore 1978
Eleanor Jones 1980
Carolyn Bray 1985
Dr. Philip J. Dixon 1988
Dr. Hoover Ruppert 1990
Tom Janoski 1990
J. David Roberts 1993
Lynn J. Glassbrook 1997

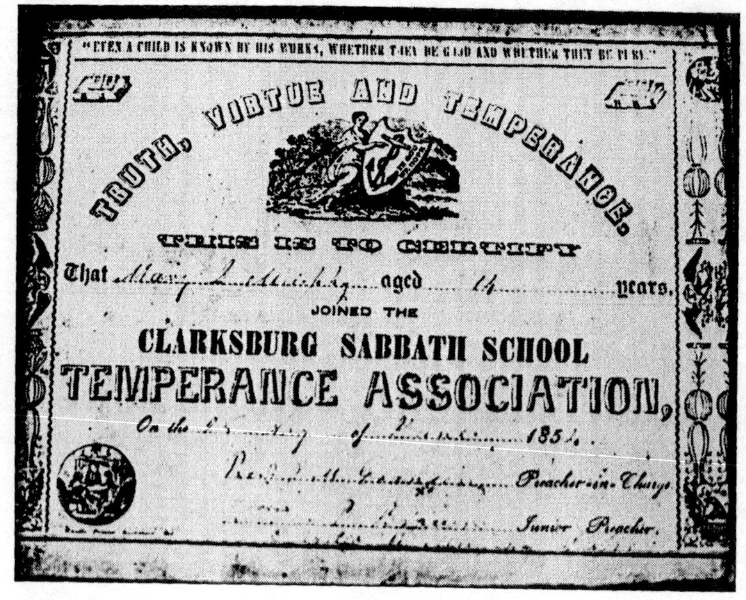

"EVEN A CHILD IS KNOWN BY HIS WORKS, WHETHER THEY BE GOOD AND WHETHER THEY BE PURE."

TRUTH, VIRTUE AND TEMPERANCE.

THIS IS TO CERTIFY

That [illegible] aged 14 years,

JOINED THE

CLARKSBURG SABBATH SCHOOL

TEMPERANCE ASSOCIATION,

On the [illegible] day of [illegible] 185[illegible].

[illegible] Preacher-in-Charge.

[illegible] Junior Preacher.

Mary J. Appleby's 1854 Certificate

54. Arthur Gibson House

The original house was owned by Georgiana G. Hackey and was built in 1918. The house was sold to Arthur M. and Ella Hackey Gibson on September 29, 1924. After the house burned they lived in the small house until the house was rebuilt. Built to the original specifications, the two-story house is three bays by on bay and has two brick end chimneys. There is a single story addition in the rear. The front porch roof is supported by four square posts. The roof is covered with raised seam metal. The house was sold to Mrs. Gibson's nephew, Arthur Randall and then to Frank Dorsey.

55. site of Clarke Farm

Home of the town's founder, John Clarke lived here with his wife Ann Archey Clarke. Today the land is a popular recreation spot and King's Pond has even been used for baptisms. The property was later owned by Raymond King, then Howard Montgomery Miles, Jr., then Fred Cushman. The Clark(e) Family Cemetery is located here. The stones were removed and are stored in the Little Bennett Park office but will be re-set in the town center park. The stones read: One with no inscription, #2 S. Bell, #3 Ann Clark wife of John Clark, Esquire d. 27 March 1810 in her 61st year, "Sacred forever may this place be made, My Father and Mother's humble shaid, Unmov'd and undisturb'd till time shal end, The turf that's round them may God defend." #4 Gustarvus Wilson was born 11th Feb 1811 and departed 23rd day of the same month, William Harris: In Memory of The amiable, affectionate and pious Mr. William Harris nephew and adopted Son of Rev'd Buckley Carl pastor of the Presbyterian Church in Rahway New Jersey departed this life ___b. 5th 1____; _____of Divine ____e; and John Clark inscription illegible. In 1848 the 'Clarksburg Turnpike' was constructed. Beginning at the Methodist Church, it wound it's way through the Layton, Soper and Beall properties. The following men were paid for their services: Edward Lewis, commissioner — two days $4.00; Obed. Hurley — two days $4.00; Nicholas Worthington, surveyor and platter — $7.00; Arnold T. Lewis — one day $1.00; Howard Lewis — one day $1.00; Richard Umstead, poleman — $1.00; James T. Henning, axman — $1.00; Eli Wolfe, J.P. administered oaths — 43 3/4 cents. The following landholders were each paid one cent as a token for damages to their property: William Wilson, M. E. Church, Charles Hill Murphy, William Layton, John L. Layton, John L. Soper, William Beall and Basil Beall. John L. Tyson received $10.00. On May 10, 1952 the King Community Lake was dedicated on the site of the former farm.

56. House at Snowden's corner

The two-story frame house was built in 1890 for Clifton H. and Rachel Snowden. The original, center section has a stone foundation and there is a center brick chimney. The gable roof has two windowed dormers, and sections have been added to both ends of the house. The house is presently covered with siding. Following the death of their son Jack, the Snowden's took in foster children, one of whom was William C. Hammond who resided here and then built the house next door. The hill beyond this home is known as Musgrove Hill. At the intersection of Burnt Hill Road and Piedmont Road once the house of Jerome and Nancy Lyddard. It was later occupied by his son, John C. Lyddard, wife Mary Emma Lyddard and family.

57. Snowden Farm

This property was purchased by Thomas Snowden from James Henning Pudum on February 23, 1889. The older section of the house was built in 1889 and later that year Mrs. Lydia Snowden died. The house is located on Piedmont Road, just outside of Clarksburg. After marrying Henrietta J. Snowden an addition was completed c. 1900. One of the children of this marriage was Franey R. Snowden. The farm was conveyed to Franey and Madessa O. Snowden. They raised foster children here, two of whom were Leona and Charles Pendleton. Leona married Calvin H. Fitz and the farm was conveyed to them in the 1950's. Calvin Fitz, Jr. presently owns the property.

Burdette Road Farms
58. Burdette Farm

Piedmont Road was formerly called Burdette Road. This two-story frame house is an example of the houses in this vicinity. It is three bay by one bay and was built for Hamilton and Elizabeth R. King Burdette. Elizabeth was a daughter of William and Delilah Miles King. The fish scale detailing in the center gable is accented by a diamond shape window. The corregated metal roof and full-length front porch are typical features of Maryland farmhouses. The front porch roof is supported by turned posts. There are presently two styles of chimney, a center brick and a stove pipe. After Hamilton Burdette retired and moved to Boyds, his daughter and son-in-law purchased the farm. Martha Rebecca Burdette married James Henning Purdum in 1871 and died in 1883. Purdum then married Sarah Edith Lewis. He divided the farm by selling a parcel to Thomas Snowden and part to his son-in-law Elias Vinson King. His son James F. Purdum lived here from the 1920's until he sold the property to his son James William "Bill" Purdum. Following his death the farm was sold out of the family.

59. Purdum House

Built c. 1905 for James F. Purdum and Nellie Estelle Burdette Purdum, this house was part of the James Henning Purdum farm. Later families to live here included the Scotts and the Summers who had a strawberry patch here in the 1940's. The house is a two-story three bay facade with a gable roof. The center gable is ornately decorated with jig saw work. The shed roof porch is supported by four columns and there are two brick interior chimneys. The house faces Piedmont Road.

60. Windsor Farm

Another area farm was that of William R. Windsor. The Windsor family cemetery is located on the property. Brother Windsor married Annie E. Murphy, daughter of Charles Hill Murphy and Julia Ann Richardson Murphy. Brother Windsor was active in the Clarksburg Methodist Church and was a charter member of the Clarksburg I. O. O. F. The house has a log section and an addition and pre-dates 1879. The farm is presently owned by Robert Tregoning.

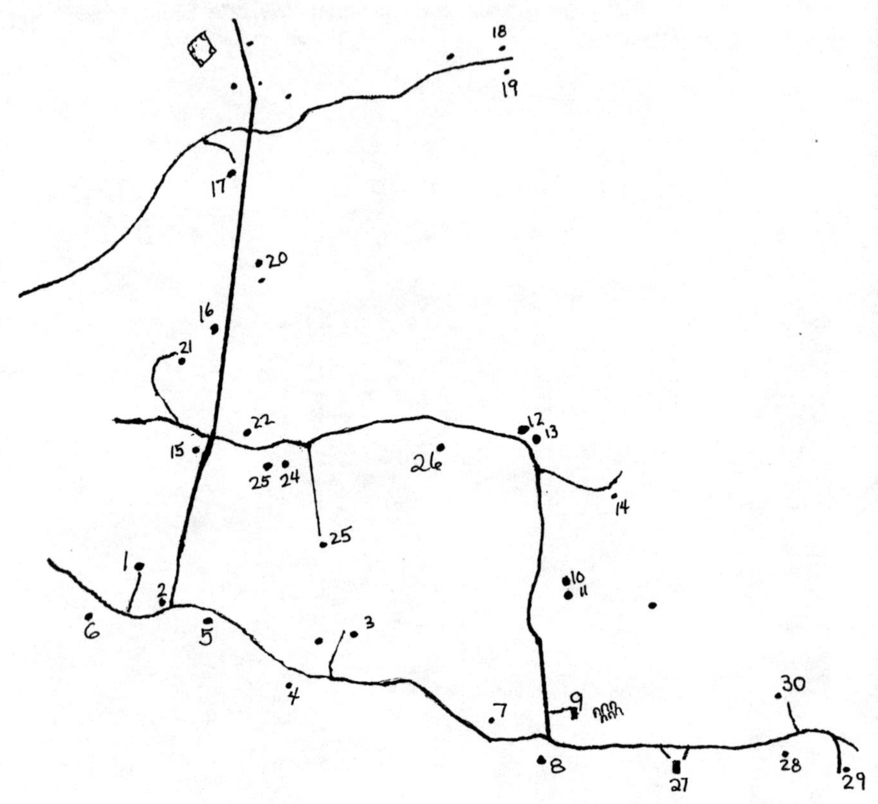


**Map of King's Valley**

## Chapter Three
## King's Valley

The land that forms King's Valley is now partly a section of Little Bennett Regional Park. When the park was being developed buildings that were not up to county code were burned. This included the cabin of "Aunt" Nancy Jackson, the farm houses of John Ashton, the former Snowden Farm later Jimmy Burdette's farm, Charles Picquett, Eli Garrett Cooley, John Grimes, John E. Grimes, John P. Lawson, Oscar Meyer, Rebecca Norwood, the Loys, Huertas, Waltons, Molinex, Nickrows, Browns and others. The home of Robert and Matilda Marshall is still standing, although it is not presently occupied. The school building was saved and is located on one of the park trails.

John Duckett King and John Snowden were two of the earliest property owners in the area. The descendants of John Duckett King prospered in the valley named for their family. His son Luther Green King organized the King's Valley Band. Luther Green King was a former member of the Clarksburg Band and Frank King has several of the instruments in his possesion. John A. King became a blacksmith, an essential occupation, not only for shoeing horses, but for everything from nails to trivets. In 1860 the Constable for the area was Green G. Waters. King's Valley did not have it's own post office and most of the families received their mail in Clarksburg, although some received it from Purdum or Damascus. Pictured below is the King's Valley Band c. 1900. Among other events it is recalled that they played at Froggy Hallow School picnics. Front row (left to right): "Toots" Windsor, Sherman Mullinix, Joe Williams, Philip King, William Thompson. Back row: Genoa King, Albert Picquett, Rufus King, Zach Page, Luther G. King, Edward W. King and Middleton Newton King.

King's Valley Band

When Burnt Hill Road was created, the road plat of 1873 shows that the following people lived along the road and were paid for property damages and expenses: James Wilkerson Day .01, Heirs of Mrs. Thompson $25.00, Obediah Stillwell Layton .01, Catherine Rine Beall $5.00, Rufus King $60.00, C. W. King $50.00, Comissioners $140.02, Johnson Benson 3 days $6.00, Horace Waters 3 days $6.00, Richard R. Green 2 days $2.00, John T. Warfield, Sr. $8.00; Obediah Stillwell Layton, chainman, $1.25; Rufus F. King, chainman, $1.25; C. H. King, poleman $1.25; James Wilkerson Day, axman $1.25; W. A. $169.02. In September 1885 the road was improved. Living along the road at that time were S. A. Richards, Charles T. Browning, John N. Soper, James S. Buxton, Leonidas Willson, John P. Lawson, Obediah S. Layton, James Wilkerson Day, Anna L. Robertson. The road crew consisted of John P. Sellman, examiner; John Lyddard, examiner; William Williams, examiner; R. W. Benton, chainman; G. S. Stone, chainman; Benjamin F. Hawkins, axman; Richard H. Bowman, rodman; C. F. Townsend, surveyor.

View of Price's Distillery Road

## Residences and Buildings in King's Valley

1. Watkins Farm

This was the farm of Henry Gue in 1879 and was part of "Prospect Hill". The left side of the house is the original section, and has a stone chimney. The right section is also of log and has a dirt basement. Both sections were built in the early 1800's. Later the house was covered with siding. Leroy Webster and Bessie Lee King Watkins purchased the farm in 1918 and the barn was built in 1922. They built and occupied a house on a section of the 78 acres which was a parcel of the King farm. The farm was conveyed to their son, William King Watkins who sold it recently.

2. Claude King House

The frame house is two-stories with three bays and a rear one-story addition. The shed roof porch is supported by four square posts. The land was originally a portion of the Edward J. King farm. Lewis Bell King and Emma Jane Hurley King moved here after they sold their farm. He was a carpenter who carried his tools on his back, and also a son of Edward J. King and Mary Jane Burdette King. The house was later owned by Claude H. King and Oda May Cline King. On August 29, 1936 he sold the property to Thurston B. King.

3. Edward J. King House

This land is part of "Trouble Enough Indeed" and had an old log house behind the present house which is now gone. The present two-story frame house was built in 1905 from timber on the property and has a gable roof and an interior chimney. The facade gable has an arched window with returned cornices. The front porch roof is supported by turned columns. The house has not had any major renovations and appears much the same as it did nearly one hundred years ago. This house was conveyed to Garrett Webster Watkins and then to his son Wilbur Noah Watkins. The house is presently owned by his William King Watkins. Behind the King house was a log house which is no longer standing. Beside this house once stood the house of John Elmon Beall, which is also gone.

4. Ira King House

This house was built for Rinaldo Delaney King and his wife Mary S. Ward King c. 1918 and the property was parceled from Charles Miles King's farm. They sold it to Thomas King and his wife Oner Della Hilton King. Ira Leroy King, their son, later purchased the property from Julian P. King in 1933. Ira's son, Sterling King, lived here subsequently. The house is an American Four-square with a hipped roof and a wrap around porch. The brackets for the porch roof on the facade are jig saw work.

5. Thurston King House

This was the site of F. 'Scott' King and Elizabeth E. Williams King's house which was built c. 1876. The property was part of "Genoa" and part of "Dorsetshire". Prior to moving to the Tomahawk Farm, Thurston King's homeplace was this two-story three bay by one bay frame house built c. 1911. He was a son of Holiday Hix King and Amy Jane Musgrove King. The house has a three bay facade and a center doorway. The unusual half-round window on the second floor adds to the charm of the house. The full-length front porch has a shed roof supported by turned posts. There was another house next to this one where George Gray lived, and a house across the road where the Snowdens lived. Both houses are no longer standing.

6. Bradley Warfield House

This was the home of Bradley Warfield. The roof is presently covered with corrigated metal and the facade has a center gable in the gable roof. The present owner is Jean E. Myers. Near here was another house, where Marshall Snowden lived. The Yokleys' were tenants here in the 1950's and the house was burned as a drill for the Hyattstown Fire Department in the 1970's.

7. William Edward King House

Original house on this site was built c. 1880 and burned in 1919. William's father, Charles Miles King conveyed this land to him after his marriage to Anna Temple Burdette. William married Addie Mae Brown in 1920, and they raised their family in this two-story three bay frame house, which was rebuilt in 1919. The gable roof has a center gable facade with an arched window. Two interior chimneys provide heat for the house. The foundation is of stone and several log outbuildings are well preserved on the property.

8. Young and King's Store

The intersection has been drastically altered over the years, necessitating the removal of the section of the building in which the store was located. Originally, the road passed the store and Kingstead Road ended where the lane to the farm is presently located. When Kingstead Road was graded and the embankment was needed, the store was demolished. The two-story three bay frame house is still located on this site, but after several remodeling projects no longer resembles this charming scene. On January 31, 1825 the property and house were sold by John Duckett King to George W. Fletchall and John Young, who operated Fletchall and Young's store here. Thomas Young and Charlotte Lewis Young were in partnership with the Kings in 1860, but had moved by 1870. Pictured below are Luther N. King, daughter Lucille Clara King and wife Clara Mullineaux King.

9. Charles Miles King House

The first log house on this property, built c. 1840, with a stone chimney is no longer standing. The now L-shaped frame house was built c. 1873 with a two-story five bay facade and a full length front porch. The house is eccletic with center chimneys and end chimneys. There is a family cemetery behind the barn were John Duckett and Jemima Miles King are presumed to be buried along with other family members. The cemetery is noted on the plat in 1887 as Grave Yard Lot for the partition of the estate of Charles Miles King. The tracts were: "Part of Hope Improved," "Trouble Enough Indeed," and "Timber Neck." The farm is known internationally as "Kingstead Farm."

10. Luther Green King House

The original log structure has been incorporated into the frame addition shown below. The house was part of the King property "Trouble Enough Indeed" designated as the Luther Green King lot. He had this house built in 1899 when he married Mary Lorena King. It was later used as the miller's house when William Franklin and and Lola Thompson lived here. William Thompson was the flour miller from 1908 until the late 1920's. The house has 1, 880 square feet and sits on 4.88 acres. In recent years John and James Clayton operated a landscaping service here. Across Kingstead Road was a lane to a log house which is now in decay.

11. King's Mill

The mill pond and mill race were here originally. Remains of the old race are mostly obliterated, but they were located in the meadow beyond the hill. Pictured below is the grist mill with William Appleby standing in the doorway. John Snowden had owned acreage in the area, and the mill was sold by him to the King family. The complex also included a saw mill and cider mill. The road in the foreground once extended from Kingstead Road to Price's Distillery Road. Along this road was Elmon G. Burdette's farm. His wife's mother, Hannah Ann King Burdette was a daughter of John Duckett King. His land was purchased from Luther M. Browning on July 3, 1849.

12. King Log House

One of the early log houses built for Luther Green King was this one, which was located near the distillery. It was three bay by one bay and probably had a small front porch. The foundation was of local fieldstone, as the house was near the creek. It was later covered with sheathing and a wrap around porch was added. Roby Harriman Brown and his wife Virgie Estelle Price Brown were the last people living on the property before the house burned.

13. King's Distillery

Luther Green King owned and operated the King's Distillery. Area farms grew rye which was distilled into whiskey here. The bottle pictured below was in the collection of the late Roby H. Brown. When he farmed here, he used the old warehouse for produce storage before trucking it to the Florida Avenue market in Washington, D. C.

14. John Brewer King Farm

Two-story three bay by one bay frame house has two brick chimney and the front porch roof is supported by turned posts. The balustrade runs the length of the porch, which has been remodeled to extend down the side of the house and the older log section. The roof is covered with raised seam metal and several lightening rods are perched atop the roof. Until recently the farm still raised tobacco. In more recent years this was the home of Basil Russell Glaze and Bertie May King Glaze. Presently, their son John Russell Glaze lives here. The road used to connect from Price's Distillery Road to Kingstead Road, near the site of the former distillery.

Along Kingsley Road
15. Robertson-King House

This was the property of George and Anna L. Robertson. In 1900 Nonie M. Lyddard and Edward Carlton King purchased the house and land. Subsequently the old summer kitchen was connected to the rear of the main house. The old log house was sheathed with siding more recently. The two-story house is three bays by two bays and the front porch hipped roof is supported by posts with lattice work. There is a brick chimney in both sections of the house.

16. Kingsley School

George Robertson, Anna L. Robertson, Grafton and Nellie E. Duvall sold an acre of ground from "Layton's Inheritance" for Froggy Hollow School, later called "Kingsley." The property was undesirable, being in the hollow, and was purchased for $2.00. Nearby the Little Bennett Creek babbles under a swaying foot bridge that at one time was just a wooden plank for students to cross. Built on a fieldstone foundation, the one room school measures 22 feet by 32 feet with twelve foot ceilings. It was constructed for $399.19. Four tall windows, now boarded up, lit the classroom. Until the mid 1920's three windows were located on the opposite wall, too. However they were boarded up during a renovation. The platform for the teacher's desk was also removed at this time. Oil-kerosene lamps with reflectors were added about this time. A bell hung in the roof, which had an indoor rope for the teacher to signal the beginning of the school day. The school opened on September 1, 1893 with 28 students. A pot bellied stove heated the school, with a single flue chimney. A slate chalkboard of 63 square feet provided workspace for handwriting and mathematics. An ante-room afforded space for wraps and lunch pails. The desks were double seated with lift tops and the teacher's desk sat at the front of the room. Before the start of the school day two boys were sent to the spring for water. A Victrola provided music on a cylinder, and a globe and shelves for books were added. A water cooler was also provided. Two privies were located out back. Also behind the school in later years was the woodshed, the flag pole, and the dirt road. The playgroung was an open space between the creek and the school. Baseball and Dodge ball were favorite games. Another recess activity indulged in by some of the older boys was a trip to Nancy Jackson's house for some 'hard cider.' The teacher was informed and moved the desks of the partaker up beside the stove, which gave the class a lesson in the amplified effects of imbibibing such liquids. Over the years the school janitors were Ed King, Woodrow Cooley, and Tom Oden. Lewis Bell King was a Trustee.

At 9:00 the teacher rang the bell, and students lined up single file. The Victrola was wound and a march began for the students to enter the building. Students greeted their teacher, recited the Lord's Prayer and Pledge of Allegiance, and took their seats after the flag was raised. Spelling bees were a regular part of the school day. At 10:00 students had a fifteen minute morning recess, and then continued their studies until noon. In winter months the teacher occasionally prepared soup on the stove. At 2:00 the students had afternoon recess and then continued class until 4:00. Fund raisers for the school included an Oyster Supper. Students decorated the school for Christmas but did not have any plays or entertainments. On the last day of school students were treated to ice cream and strawberries. Most students were sent to Clarksburg when Kinglsey closed. The property was sold to Bertha Cooley in 1936 for $300.00. The Little Bennett Park planned to maintain the building as a museum, and used it for instruction until it was vandalized in the 1970's. Currently Maryland-National Capital Park and Planning Commission owns the building.

Some of the students were Madeline King, Marion King, Kenneth King, Archie Hood, Delma Hood, Myrtle Hood, Lillian King, Sherwood King, Mildred King, Carlton King, Mary King, Earl King, Esther King, Frances King, Ida Mae Grimes, James B. Grimes, John E. Grimes, Jr., Thomas Grimes, and William H. Grimes.

Teachers:

| | |
|---|---|
| Willis O. Rhodes | 1893-1900 |
| Kate Murphy | 1900-1908 |
| Katie Ricketts | 1908-1910 |
| Laura Jenkins | 1910-1914 |
| Anice Julia Murphy | 1914-1917 |
| Mary Lowe Smith | 1917-1920 |
| Maude Ashton | 1920-1928 |
| Mrs. Elsie Pearson Green | 1928-1931 |
| Maude Ashton | 1931-1934 |

Many of the teachers boarder with Eli Garrett Cooley and his family, whose property adjoined the school.

17. site of Grimes House

The top photograph shows a house that is no longer standing. It was off Clarksburg Road on the portion of Hyattstown Mill - Kingsley Road which is closed. The property was purchased from Isaac S. Henry in 1888 and the house dates to that time. In 1893 Mr. Grimes purchased additional land from Maria E. Willson. The bottom picture was taken during slaughtering time.

18. Marshall House

Entering Hyattstown Mill Road from Clarksburg Road one would have passed the houses of the Buxton family and Jim and Altha Wims, the fence and foundation are still visible, and across in the meadow was the ballfield where the Wildcat's played. The Maryland Wildcats won 37 games in an undefeated season and had two players, Chuck Henton and Sonny Jackson, who became professional ball players. Returning to Clarksburg Road one passes the site of Lee Wilson's saw mill and the site of the Loy house. Continuing up the hill on the left was the site of Charlotte Henry's home and after cresting the hill, the Marshall house is on the left. Robert Marshall purchased this property after it was foreclosed. The house of William Brown once sat closer to the road, and is no longer standing. The present two-story frame house has been covered with siding. The facade is two bays with a center door. The chimney is of block construction. The house has been unoccupied since Stella Marshall died.

19. site of Bethel Chapel

Bethel Methodist Protestant Chapel served the families of King's Valley and Lewisdale. It was built of log and of the same specifications as the Mt. Lebanon Chapel near Damascus. Several interments were in the cemetery, and after the church closed, the tombstones were moved to Bethesda Methodist Cemetery in Browningsville. The structure was moved to Fountain Mills in Frederick County, Maryland. The road bed is still visible across Clarksburg Road from the Marshall house. Annual picnics were held across the road in Loy's Grove for the benefit of the church each August. Music was provided by local bands and programs of recitations and speeches were scheduled. One December 14, 1904 Rev. J. H. Mullinix gave a lecture at the church after returning from the Holy Land. He brought with him artifacts and many pictures.

20. site of Ashton Farm

John A. Ashton and his wife Emily Lee Mills Ashton moved here from Virginia. He bought part part of the tract called "Resurvey on Blanford". Their son, John Wesley Ashton, married Susan Elizabeth Lawson, a neighbor. John A. Ashton sold land to Lillian Lawson, John Wesley Ashton, Horace D. Waters, William Brown and Dominic Naples. The John Ashton farm was sold to Jimmy Burdette and subsequently to the Beechers. The house was destroyed by fire in 1964. The large barn was considered as a possible site for horse stables in the 1980's, but the structure was taken down. Their daughter Maude Ashton taught at Kingsley and Browningsville schools. At the bottom of the hill on Kingsley Road was the quarry. Also along this section was the store and residence of John P. Lawson c. 1895 - 1910. All of these sites are located in Little Bennett Regional Park.

21. Tomahawk Farm

James Edward Day and Emma Jane Lawson Day purchased this land, "Belt's Tomahawk", from James Wilkerson Day and the house pictured below was built in 1880. The two-story frame house was five bays by two bays and had a gable roof with center gable facade. Two exterior brick chimneys flanked the older section of the house, and another was located in the rear ell. The outbuildings created a picturesque vista from road. In 1928 Thurston B. King and Pomona Burdette King purchased the farm. When Donald Pleasants purchased the property he re-named it Tomahawk Farm, and had the farm house replaced by the present modern home. The house faced Burnt Hill Road.

22. James Hood House

This land is part of "Ebenezer" and part of "Layton's Inheritence." The original house on this property was of log and sat behind the present house. The log house was the home of Obediah Stillwell Layton, and his wife, Sarah N. King Layton, whom he married in 1852. The log house was taken down in the mid-1920's. The present house was built for James O. Hood and Lena Jane King Hood in 1921. The house originally had three bedrooms, a parlor and a dining room. The back porch was later enclosed for a kitchen. The mantel and mirror in the parlor were ordered from Sears Roebuck and picked up at Boyds Station with the Hood name stamped on them. Under the parlor is a root cellar and the house has a stone foundation. James O. Hood farmed here and after his death in 1972 the property was conveyed to Donald and Jeannie Mae Mullineaux Raines who have a tenant here presently. The house faces Burnt Hill Road.

23. Walden King Farm

In 1756 Edward Browning owned a portion of this land. Another portion was originally part of "Layton's Inheritence." The present house is perched on a hill and was originally built of logs with a three bay facade. The loft upstairs was accessed by a ladder. Walden Vincent King moved here with his wife, Violena Shipley King, in 1915 when the frame section had been built. They owned the land on both sides of Burnt Hill Road, grew tobacco and rye for the King's Distillery. In the 1940's the family had a truck patch farm, growing a variety of vegetables to sell in the Women's Market in Bethesda. Violena King also took baked goods to the market. They also raised poultry, and had a cow for milk and butter. In 1944 the rear addition was added to the house. In 1958 a brick house was built on the property for their granddaughter, Eloise Haney Woodfield and her husband Thomas L. Woodfield. In 1969 the fields were planted in corn and wheat, and Jersey cows grazed in the meadow. In 1989 the family re-named the property Kae-Lee Farm and it is a horse farm presently run by the Woodfields. This farm received the Maryland Century Farm Award in 1999. It has been in the same family for 245 years and is a working farm today.

24. Haney House

This house was built by Forrest Norwood Haney and Carlton King for Forrest and his wife Mary Esther King Haney in 1936. Their daughter, Eloise Haney Woodfield, was born here. The front porch has been enclosed. After 1945 when the Haney's moved, several renters were in the house. One was Selina Caldor whose brother Louie came from New York to live with her. He had 'discovered' Grandma Moses' art talent. The house faces Burnt Hill Road and is a parcel of the Walden King farm.

25. Hix King Farm

Originally the farm of John Wesley Beall and Catherine Rine Beall, this property was part of "Prospect Hill". John died in 1866, and Catherine lived here with her son, John Elmon Beall, who married Sommerville W. King. He later built a house on Stringtown Road, down the hill from this farm. In 1898 Holiday Hix King and Reuben Kephart divided this section of the property. The Kephart house is no longer standing, but this house was purchased in 1963 by the late Reno Continetti. Ann Continetti, his widow, lives there presently.

26. King - Beall House

This was part of the Edward Browning property which was left to his daughter Rachel Browning Purdum and her husband Joshua Purdum. It was sold to Rufus and Amanda E. Mobley King who sold it to Daniel W. Price who married Sarah F. Howard. The was property was conveyed to his son-in-law Melvin Beall who married Eva M. Price on August 27, 1912. The house is a two-story frame house with a three bay facade. The gable roof has a center gable facade. The windowed gable and end gables have returned cornices. There is an external brick chimney. The bank barn is also visible to the right of the house. In the early 1950's Edgar Riedel purchased the property from Melvin Beall and his daughter, Kathleen Riedel Cumberledge, is the present owner.

27. King's Valley Schoolhouse

In 1869 three quarters of an acre was purchased from Charles M. King for $15.00 to build a school. Luther M. Watkins was the first teacher in 1869 here, however, Joseph J. Benson was teaching students in the vicinity by 1860. The school was insured for $300 in 1883 and received new desks in 1890. An addition was built in 1894 at a cost of $150. Julia Helen King was the teacher c. 1893 - 1900. In 1900 the school received a new floor and was then being called "Day's" School. Teachers were Columbus Washington Day and Jerry Burdette. The school pictured below burned in 1908, and a new building was erected on the same site in 1909. In 1915 the school was reportedly overcrowded. Blanche Willard Walker was the teacher in 1915, Ola Burdette taught here in 1929. Former students recall that they had single desks, swings, spelling bees, and learned from watching the older students. Boys helped bring in wood from the wood shed before school on winter mornings, and carried water from the stream before the well was dug. There were two recesses during the school day, and students brought their lunch from home. Games that were played at recess were Annie-over, Red-rover and dodge ball. Students included Virginia Cordell, Lorraine Hilton, Lillian Brown and Ritchie Lee Haney walked together to and from school from the Purdum area. Other students included: Forrest Haney, Thomas D. Woodfield, Harold Young, Everett Jones and Dorothy Hilton In 1935 the school was closed and the building was torn down with the materials used for repairing other buildings in the vicinity. The property reverted back to the heirs of the King farm.

Students of King's Valley School

King's Valley Students, 1931 Back row (Left to right): Louise Poole, Millard Burdette, Jr., Violet Beall, Janice Burdette, Lorraine Hilton, Lillian Brown and Helen Belle Shipley. Front row: Elwood Wright, Earl Wright, John Glaze, Lindsey Thompson, Earl Glaze, Hilton Nehouse, Carl Stephens, Glenwood King, William King, Maurice King, James Stephens and Deets Beall.

28. Jones House

Ira L. and Ursula King Jones purchased this property in 1912 from Genoa King. The two-story three bay facade frame house has a gable roof and center gable facade. The roof of the front porch is supported by tapered columns and the roof is of raised seam metal. The house was built in 1912 and is presently owned by the heirs of Leslie King. Currently the Lakes reside here.

29. Hilton Farm

According to land records this was purchased from Snowden by Thomas Hilton. The land went to his son and daughter-in-law, John Brice Hilton and Sarah Elizabeth Brown Hilton. The property was conveyed to their son Grover Hilton and was subsequently purchased on June 30, 1920 by Ernest G. Hilton, son of Grover Hilton. The house was built c. 1880 and is a two-story frame house with two interior brick chimneys. There is a two-story rear ell and a full-length front porch. The house is presently abandoned and a new house has been built beside it. The old log tabacco house is no longer standing. Upon the death of Ernest Hilton in 1999, the farm was willed to his sister, Lorraine Hilton Liski who sold it to Chester Leishear.

Tobacco and corn on Hilton Farm

Winter on the Hilton Farm

Ernest Hilton drove a school bus in the 1930's

30. Rufus King House

The adjoining property was the Rufus Fillmore King farm. He married Ursala Mahala King in 1874, both were descendants of John Duckett King. Rufus S. King had this house built on a parcel of the farm c. 1910. The two-story frame house had a gable roof with Victorian influences. The house was heated by a central brick chimney. The porch's shed roof was supported by four columns. The rear porch roof was similar. The house had a basement, stone foundation and was abandoned in the 1970's when this photograph was taken. The house is no longer standing.

## The History of Purdum

Purdum is a small, rural community located in northern Montgomery County, Maryland. John Purdum, one of the early land owners, lived at the intersection of the two existing roads, and it is thought that the area was named for him. In the early part of the nineteenth century it was largely agricultural, being part of the tobacco growing region. The historical district contains late nineteenth and early twentieth century buildings along Price's Distillery Road between Johnson Drive and Purdum Road. In the early to mid-nineteenth century there was no commercial development, only the scattered farms of Thomas Brown, John Purdum, Luther Browning, John Middleton King, Gabriel Lewis Duvall "Dick" Lawson, Harry Hurley and George White. Much of the land was part of the tract "Trouble Enough Indeed" which was granted to Thomas Whitten in 1761. The Pleasant Plains schoolhouse was between the King and White farms. In 1869 the Pleasant Grove schoolhouse was built to serve the black community.

In 1875 the Methodist Protestant class, which had been meeting in the Pleasant Plains school, built the church and formed their own congregation. A cemetery was established next to the church. Directly behind the church was the land of Thomas G. Brown which he named "Cedar Grove." A blacksmith shop was located beside the cemetery. In 1889 William Alfred Smith was appointed as post master and locals could pick up their mail in his general store. On July 27, 1907 the mail service was moved to Monrovia and presently comes from Damascus.

When Delaney Floyd Brown opened a general store, Purdum became self-sufficient. Mr. Brown also huckstered, exchanging farm goods for wares they needed. The remaining farms are cattle and dairy operations.

Purdum, like the other communities, had a band. It was organized in the 1920's and performed at area picnics and held an annual carnival in the woods on the late Guy Johnson's property. Events included the milk-bottle knockdown, wheel of chance and a mile run. Outdoor chicken dinners were also served. The members pictured below are (left to right): Ritchie E. Haney, Harry G. Hurley, Woodrow "Mann" Brown, Eugene French, Roby H. Brown, Roby T. Beall, C. Brooks Beall, Edward W. King, William Thompson, Arthur W. Beall, Willett S. King, Delaney F. Brown, Dorsey Brown, John D. King, and Middleton N. King. The scene on the bass drum was painted by Rev. Frank E. Volk, pastor of the Mt. View Church from 1924 - 1927.

The Damascus ball team played on the field behind the Smith house. Pictured below is the 1926-27 team. Front row (left to right): Guy Watkins, Paul Wire, "Horsemeat" Cook, Carl Snapp, Harold Burdette. Back row: Lawrence Luhn, Les Barber, Phil Purdum, Ed King, Roy Purdum, Bake Selby and Guy Hurley. The photograph was taken at McCurdy field in Frederick when Damascus was playing against the Frederick Hustlers.

The baseball diamond was also used by the Damascus High School team from 1930 until 1940. Afterward a home field was built in Damascus.

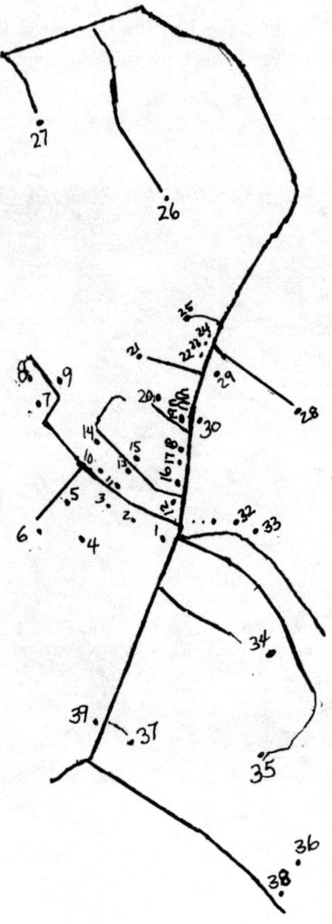


**MAP OF PURDUM**

## Houses and Buildings in Purdum

1. Beall - Smith House

This house was built for Eli Beall c. 1888 and he and his wife Martha lived here. After their death their daughter and son-in-law moved here. Ellsworth McCullough Smith and Addie Mae Beall Smith, both died in 1972. The two-story frame house was three bay by one bay with a two-story ell in the rear. Both sections had a gable roof. The front porch had been removed by the time this photograph was taken c. 1974. There was a ballfield in back and a cornfield beyond. The house was destroyed by fire c. 1980. Notice that Purdum had a traffic circle at the intersection of Purdum Road, Price's Distillery Road and Mountain View Road.

Houses on Purdum Road
2. Beall - Poole House

This house was the home of George W. and Savannah Edith Brown Beall. Mrs. Beall was a daughter of Thomas G. Brown and Catherine Ann Moxley Brown. The house was built c. 1887 and has conveyed to their son-in-law, Clarence Robert Poole. Mr. Poole was married to Lillie Mae Beall and later Dora Irene Beall. The one-story frame house has been remodeled and covered with siding. Mr. Gregg now lives in this house. Down the unused lane near this house was the farm of Lorenzo Dow Watkins and his wife Airy Ann Watkins.

3. Day House

This two-story three bay by one bay frame house has a gable roof and pipe-style chimney. It was built by Mr. Nichols of Clarksburg in 1939 for Frank Day. The wrap around porch roof is supported by posts. Frank Day lived here with his son, Joseph Harold Day until his death. Mamie Dorsey Day Mullinix lived here with her brother after her husband died. The house was sold to Walter Siering who has remodeled house, improved the property and resides there presently.

4. King Homeplace

This farm on "Resurvey of Long Looked For" has been parceled into several properties. The oldest house was built for George Edward King and his wife, Julia Ann Burdette King c. 1862 on property he purchased from Lorenzo D. Watkins. He was a grandson of John Duckett King and Jemima Miles King. Following his death in 1876 Julia married his brother, Zadoc Summers King and the farm was divided among his children in 1893. One of the parcels was inherited by Nicholas Edward and Laura Gerturde King Burns who built a house on the property at that time. Pictured below are (left to right) John Middleton King, Zadoc King, Amanda King, Julia Ann Burdette King and Edward King. The house was of log construction with a five bay facade and two exterior stone chimneys. The full-length front porch had a shed roof supported by posts and a portion of the porch was enclosed. The photograph was taken c. 1900.

5. Middleton King House

This house was built for Middleton Newton King c. 1900. An additon was constructed by his son, Harvey Webster King, in 1942, who lived here with his wife Pauline Burdette King. The two-story frame house is five bays by two bays with a gable roof. The facade's center gable has an arched window and returned corners. There are two brick interior chimneys. The roof is covered with corrugated metal as is the porch roof, which is supported by bracketed posts. The porch has an attractive balustrade. Frank A. "Chubby" King, Marjorie King and Violet King grew up here. Edward J. Flynn lives here presently.

6. King Farm

Following the division of the George Edward King farm in 1893, Middleton Newton King, inherited this portion and after he retired the farm was conveyed to his son, Harvey Webster King. The first section of the house was a three bay facade log house, which was later extended to the present structure. The full-length front porch has been enclosed. A Dutch hipped-roof barn was built in the 1940's. When Harvey King retired from farming he traded the farm for the Victorian-style house and the Chiles family lived in the farm house. The Toth family was the last to farm here. An adjoining farm that of Edward Walter King and his wife Fannie D. Dutrow King. The farm was conveyed to their children: John Dutrow King, Edward Ray King, William Taft King, Amanda Marie King and Nora Bell King Watkins. Edward Walter King was a son of George Edward and Julia Ann Burdette King.

7. Burdette House

This is one of three houses built for Abraham Lincoln Burdette and Georgia Ellen Waters King Burdette on part of "Resurvey on Long Looked For". After he sold the farm to his son this two-story home was constructed with a gable roof extending to form the roof of the front porch which is supported by four posts. The pump remains in the front yard reminding us of a time before modern conveniences. After Linc Burdette lived here, Rinaldo Delaney and Mary Sybelle Ward King lived here, as did Walter and Sallie Stern. Ralph "Huck" Mullinix and his wife Gloria presently live here.

8. Burdette Farm

This property is a parcel of "Resurvey on Long Looked For" and was a part of the James W. Burdette land which was conveyed to Abraham Lincoln Burdette. The house was built c. 1886 when he married Georgia Ellen Waters King. Their eight children were born here. The house was later a tenant house where Lester Hawkins lived when the farm belonged to Lansdale Burdette.

9. Lansdale Burdette House

This property is part of "Resurvey on Long Looked For" and the three bay by one bay frame house was built by Howard R. Watkins for Ira Lansdale and Fannie C. Cutsail Burdette. When they moved to Damascus, they sold the property to Herbert Steele who sold it to Charles Hanford Browning and Vivian Barnes Browning. It was here that Hanford started the Browning Pool business. In 1969 the property was sold to Walter and Nancy Hughes. Nancy is a retired school teacher from Damascus Elementary School. They are the present residents.

10. Hurley Homeplace

This two-story frame house was built in 1888 for Harry Mankin Hurley and Rosa Etta Brown Hurley. It has a three bay facade with a gable roof and center gable facade with returned cornices. The property is part of "Resurvey on Long Looked For". It was the home of their grandson, Gilmore Edward Hurley, and his wife Annie Lauretta Brandenburg Hurley before they moved to Damascus. The home is still owned by Hurley descendants and rented to tenants.

11. Borrovich Home

On this site the foundation of a store were prepared and it was decided to build the store on Mt. View Road instead. The two-story house is three bay by one bay with porches front and back, and a rear ell with a porch. The shed rooves on the porches are supported by turned posts and the house is covered with asbestos siding. The house was constructed using timber and materials from an old barn, giving it an appearance of being older than it is. It was built by Harry M. Hurley for his sister, Janie Hurley Borrovich. Her husband died in the Spanish-American War and she moved here soon afterward. In the wing, which has been demolished, she boarded Harry G. and Bessie Virginia Warthen Hurley, who upon Mrs. Borrovich's death in 1930 purchased the house. It was rented to Tommy Easton, Ralph Watkins, Mr. O'Hare and Ellwood Franklin. Guy Hurley purchased the home and he and his wife, Josephine Beall Hurley lived here. The present owner is G. Irvin Hurley.

12. Brown-Day House

This house and property were sold by George White to Catherine A. Brown in November, 1877 for $20. The property is a parcel of "Resurvey on Long Looked For". After her death, her heirs conveyed it to Richard Jefferson Brown in September 1905. Mr. Brown resided here until his death in November, 1932. His widow, Lula Blanche Poole Brown and daughter Lillian lived here. Lillian married Richard Marvin Day in 1942 and they purchased the house in May of 1951. Following his death, Lillian moved to Shady Grove.

Old Purdum Road
13. Boyer Log House

The log section of the house dates to mid-nineteenth century when Columbus Boyer lived here. He resided here until his death in 1913. Roby T. Beall purchased the house and sold it to his father, Luther T. Beall. Several additions have been constructed during renovations. Presently Diego and Susan Hurley Balcells and have made the once vacant house into a livable home. A vineyard is also under cultivation on the property. Susan is a descendant of Harry Mankin and Rose Etta Brown Hurley.

14. Willett King Log House

The property is a parcel of "Resurvey on Long Looked For". The oldest section of the house was built of chinked log and is two-story. The facade has three bays and a stone chimney. The second section is frame and was the home place of Luther T. and Leathey Beall. They farmed and raised their children here: C. Brooks Beall, Virginia Beall Moxley, Effie Beall Moxley, Gertrude Beall Wright, Roby T. Beall, Sallie Beall Appleby, Arthur W. Beall and W. Dewey Beall and his sister Addie Beall who remained here with her husband Willett S. King. After their death the property was purchased by Walter E. Hains, Jr., who rented it to John and Carol Hawse. Mr. Haines subsequently sold the property to Ronald and Jodie Burner. They have recently done extensive remodeling and preserved the log section of the home.

15. Beall House

This house was built on a parcel of "Resurvey on Long Looked For" by Thomas and Mary Frances Burdette Beall and conveyed to their daughter Emma Beall, who married Brooks Beall. It was then sold to Lucille Beall Smith and is currently owned by her daughter and son-in-law. The house has a stone foundation and appears to be c. 1890. The two-story frame house is covered with asbestos siding. Willard E. and Yvonne Smith McDonald are the present owners.

Mountain View Road
16. Brown's Store

This two-story frame two bay by four bay frame store was built c. 1912 by Raymond Brown for Delaney Brown. It was built on a parcel of "Resurvey of Long Looked For". Mr. Brown also huckstered and decided to rent the store to Luther T. Beall, who, with his son Roby operated the store. Roby entered the U. S. Army during World War I and the store was then rented to Harry G. Hurley, who is listed as the merchant in the 1920 census. Subsequently Ritchie Emmanuel Haney was the merchant from 1922 until his death in 1949. Later merchants here were Bill Huff, George Mobley and the Hurleys. During this period there were gas pumps in front of the store. After the death of the Browns, the store passed to their heirs and is presently used by Bradley Construction for storage space.

Delaney F. Brown and his wagon

Store Ledger c. 1943

17. Brown House

This house was probably built by Raymond Brown for Delaney Floyd Brown and his wife Hattie Ardean Brown. The property is a parcel of "Resurvey on Long Looked For". The house is a two-story four bay by one bay with gable roof. The center gable has returned cornices. The roof is supported by bracketed turned posts and a balustrade runs the length of the porch. The exterior walls were recently covered with aluminum siding and the roof with composition shingles. There are front and back porches and a center chimney. The house was remodeled in 2000 and now is covered with aluminum siding. Bradley Construction Company is presently using the house for an office.

18. Smith House

This two-story three bay by one bay frame Victorian-style house has a gable roof with center gable facade. The porch has a roof supported by bracketed turned posts and a balustrade. There is a single window in the gable and two center brick cimney's. The house has six rooms in the original section and wings were added later. Eliza Ann Young Smith owned this property, part of "Resurvey on Long Looked For", before the house was built for her son, Jesse Edward B. Smith c. 1899. In March 1926 it was conveyed to his widow, Flora S. King Smith. Flora lived here until her death in 1952. The house was conveyed to her sons King Smith and Ed Smith. It was later conveyed to King Smith and Dorothy M. Smith. In 1963 it was purchased by William Richard Davis, Jr. and he and his parents, William Richard, Sr. and Jessie Davis lived here. It was sold subsequently to Ken Honaker.

19. Mountain View Methodist Church and Cemetery

Early church records reveal that a Sunday School Class referred to as the "Pleasant Plains" Class was meeting prior to construction of this church. The class was on the Frederick Circuit of Methodist Protestants. Services were attended by community members arriving by horse, buggy or on foot. Camp meeting was held in Monrovia under the leadership of Reverend Cochel. The land for the present church was a parcel of "Resurvey on Long Looked For". It was purchased from George and Mary White on June 12, 1875, and the cornerstone was laid eight days later. The Reverend Dr. Shermer assisted in the service that day. The sanctuary was thirty-five feet in length and the carpenter was John Mount. In 1893 the church purchased an organ. Lighting for the church was changed from kerosene to electric lights when a Delco generator was made available by Delaney F. Brown. Heating changed from wood and coal. A new roof was put on the church in 1942 and six years later an addition and basement were constructed at a cost of $1, 812,94. Lumber was donated by Lawrence Luhn, Bill Johnson, Will Beall, and Lansdale Burdette. In 1952 the front steps were enclosed and the vestibule was built by Titus Brown. Two restrooms were added at this time. In 1959 the kitchen area was renovated, mostly funded by the Community Club Award donated by Mrs. Dorothy McCoy and Mrs. Thelma Beall. The sanctuary received major renovations in 1962, and in 1969 another addition completed the present church facility. Some of the original church pews are now in use at "Beall's Grove Camp Meeting." The 1954 church marker was replaced in 1968 by Lewis Haines and Melvin Mullinix. The present marker was created by Rev. Richard A. Closson. The following are memorials and donations:
The piano was given by the United Methodist Women
Offering plates-given by the Methodist Youth Fellowship in memory of Michael Stevens
Cross and candlesticks - given by Gertrude Beall in memory of William Johnson
American Flag - given by Mr. and Mrs. Jerry Junkin in memory of Mrs. Lucy Poole King
Christian Flag - given by the Methodist Youth Fellowship
Bell - given and hung by Mr. and Mrs. Charles Roberts
Pew Bibles - given by Rev. and Mrs. Harrison Randolph
Pulpit Bible - given by Ray Smith
Pulpit Chairs were purchased from Clarksburg Methodist by W. S. C. S.
Painting of Christ - painted by Rev. Frank Volk

The adjoining cemetery became a perpetual care cemetery in 1967. The founders of the church are intered there, although Mr. and Mrs. White's graves are unmarked.

The pastors of the church have been:
Frederick Circuit - Methodist Protestant

| | |
|---|---|
| C. T. Cochel | 1874 |
| Jesse Shreve | 1878 |
| Benjamin F. Shreve | 1883 |
| A. A. Harryman | 1884 |
| E. R. McGregor | 1885 |
| E. O. Ewing | 1888 |

W. J. Floyd 1890

Kemptown Circuit - Methodist Protestant

| | |
|---|---|
| John W. Charlton | 1893 |
| Abraham D. Dick | 1895 |
| James L. Elderdice | 1897 |
| Clarence M. Cullum | 1898 |
| Charles R. Strausberg | 1901 [assistant] |
| John A. Wright | 1902 |
| Frank Clift | 1902 [assistant] |
| Howard O. Keen | 1909 |
| George H. Stockdale | 1916 |
| Alonzo Green | 1917 |
| Charles N. Alexander | 1922 |
| F. W. Siffrin | 1923 |
| Frank M. Volk | 1924 |
| Edward E. Coleman | 1928 |
| Charles E. Cummins | 1933 |
| Gilbert E. Turner | 1934 |
| Stephen Galley | 1937 |
| J. Howard Link | 1941 [assistant] |

Montgomery Circuit - United Methodist

| | |
|---|---|
| Ira W. Shindle | 1941 |
| W. D. Eye | 1942 |
| E. Kyle Sawyers | 1945 |
| Don E. Griffin | 1947 |
| Ernest L. Harrison | 1953 |
| William T. Miller | 1956 |
| Hayden L. Sparks | 1958 |

Mt. View Charge

| | |
|---|---|
| H. Eugene Lawson | 1961 |
| Harrison R. Randolph | 1970 |
| Leighton S. Bishop | 1973 |
| Ronald Fisher | 1975 |
| Carolyn J. Walton | 1976 |
| Bruce A. Jones | 1980 |
| Carolyn J. Walton | 1982 |
| Richard A. Closson | 1984 |

Mt. View - Pleasant Grove Charge

| | |
|---|---|
| Michael E. Leftwich | 1988 |
| Kenneth R. Fell | 1995 - present |

Lord's Acre Project of Mt. View Church
Eugene and Linda Lewis, Louise Haney and Harold Day

20. Haines House

Beside the cemetery in the field was the general store and post office of William Alfred Smith. He married Catherine Ann Moxley c. 1852. After the building was no longer used as a store it was rented to various tenants. The Les Carter family and Arthur Gray family lived here, followed by William and Audrey Haines. The building was destroyed by fire while they resided here in the mid-1940's. Presently William Haines' house is located behind the field. His son Jackie and daughter-in-law Terri Johnson Haines live in a house beyond this one. All were on parcels of "Resurvey on Long Looked For".

21. Brown - Beall House

The olest section of this house was built by Thomas G. Brown. He named the property "Cedar Grove" c. 1855. The two-story frame house was later added and Thomas G. Beall and Mary F. Burdette Beall were living here in 1920. Claude Hurley purchased the house for his daughter Irene and her husband Clark Hager who lived here for several years until moving to Damascus in the mid-1920's. Ritchie E. and Helen Pearce Haney rented the house from Claude Hurley until the mid-1930's and subsequently the property sold to Lee and Myrtle Day Bosley. In 1967 William "Billy" Waters purchased the property and had a new home built. The house is unoccupied at the present time. Mr. Waters operates a portable saw mill at this location. The property is a parcel of "Resurvey on Long Looked For".

22. Smith House

This house, on a parcel of "Resurvey of Long Looked For" has been significantly altered by the present owners. It was the home of Wesley R. Smith and his wife Daisy I. Price Smith c. 1910. Roby T. Beall lived here until his death in 1921 and then the Lewis family lived here in the 1940's. It was sold to Claude and Nettie Sue Wright and then to Lindsey and Hannah Balir. Presently Frank Wodoslawsky and family reside here.

23. Hackey House

The two-story three bay center section of this house has two interior chimneys and two wings have been added. It is on a parcel of "Trouble Enough". Among the owners and occupants have been Frank and Evie Hackey, The Latonas, Guy Newton Johnson, and Ted and Linda Waldron, who enlarged and remodeled the house. Since the Pleasant Grove Christian Community Church purchased the house, various occupants have lived here.

## 24. Pleasant Grove School-Christian Community Church and Cemetery

George T. White sold an acre of "Trouble Enough" to Trustees Jeremiah Mason, Benjamin A. Davis, and Howard W. Gray for $20 in 1868 to be used for a public school and church. Fund raisers were held and a donation from the Bureau of Engraving helped the members reach their goal. Lumber for the building was hauled from Frederick by John Burdette's team of horses. On September 12, 1869 "The White School House" at Burnt Hill opened. The cemetery has stones dating to 1869. After closing for lack of students in 1895 the school re-opened in 1897. In 1899 the community requested $500 for a new school, however classes were still meeting in the church until 1908. The county furnished the books and desks and carried the insurance beginning in 1913. Anna B. Miller was the teacher in 1929. When King's Valley School closed in 1935, the Purdum Community members requested that they be allowed to use the building for a school. However, the building was disassembled and used for repair work on local farm buildings. Classes at Pleasant Grove were discontinued in 1936 and the students were transported to Damascus. The Pleasant Grove Church continued until 1966 when they merged with Friendship United Methodist Church. Some of the pastors who served the church were: Rev. Bradley Johnson, J. M. Rome, Benjamin Brown, James E. Carter, P. C. Barnes, Thomas Helsey Reed, R. H. Carpenter, J. Sherman Mason, Sr., Aaron Johnson, and James Smith. In 1967 the "Pleasant Grove Christian Community Church" was founded by Rev. Alonzo O. Graham and served until his retirement in 1992. The followship hall was dedicated to him and named Graham Hall. Rev. Lawrence Bryant succeeded Rev. Graham in 1993. Following an arson fire in 1993 services were held in the neighboring Mountain View Church while repairs were made. In 1996 four additional acres were purchased for future expansion.

25. Joshua Purdum Log House

The east section of this house was a log house built for Joshua Purdum. Columbus and Amanda Warfield Purdum lived here prior in 1869. Their daughter Hepsi Gertrude Purdum married Warner F. Poole's son Reuben Poole, who lived on the adjoining farm. Other occupants include Leo and Mamie Genus and the Willoughby family. The present house incorporated the original section in with the modern addition. Martin and Geraldine Johnson Stiles live here presently. She is a descendant of Warner F. Poole.

26. Poole-Johnson Farm

This property may have been Joshua Purdum's in 1870. The aerial photograph shows the farm and house prior to 1971. The house was torn down after an arsonist burned the barn. The house was a two-story three bay frame house with gable roof and a center gable. This was Warner F. Poole's farm before it was conveyed to his son Reuben Newton Poole, whose daughter Gertrude married William Johnson. It was conveyed to their son Guy Newton Johnson. Some of the outbuildings are still standing.

27. Haney Farm

Hamilton G. Warfield built a two-story log house c. 1859 which was located off Bethesda Church Road on what is now Haney Avenue. He married Harriet C. Miller and farmed and raised his family here. Prior to 1920 Ritchie E. Haney and his wife Helen Pearce Haney purchased the property and farmed here. At that time a two-story addition with a kitchen and back porch had been constructed. In the kitchen there was a hand-pump which supplied water without leaving the house. The farm remained in their possesion, despite the fact that they did always live there, until c. 1940 when it was sold to their daughter and son-in-law, Thelma and Arthur Beall. In the 1940's Arthur and Thelma Haney Beall built a new home closer to the road, thus beginning a development containing over thirty homes. The old home fell into disrepair and one of the new homes was built very close to the site of the old home. Pictured below are Ritchie E. and Helen Pearce Haney on their wedding day.

28. Rufus King Farm

Luther Green King conveyed this parcel of land to his son Rufus Fillmore King. His mother was Tabitha Browning King, so he came from two well-established families in the area. Rufus married Ursula Mahala King and had a number of log buildings constructed on the farm which he accessed from King's Valley Road. In 1905 he sold it to his son, Genoa, and daughter-in-law Vinnie Edna Lawson King. They lived in the log house until 1906 when the two-story four bay by two bay frame house was completed. The residence has a gable roof with returned coners, a brick chimney, and a single arched four pane window in the end gable. The addition is a side ell and the porch has been enclosed with glass windows. The old lane to the farm was no longer used and has become almost indiscernable. In 1953 E. Minor Burns and Ruth Stanley Burns purchased a part of the farm. Subsequent owners were Edgar and Bessie Stephens, Charles Roberts and when John F. and Bernice Doody purchased the farm it was re-named Wyndo Farm. Mr. Doody raised registered Holsteins here. The property is a parcel of "Trouble Enough".

29. King - Crawford House

This was the site of the first school in Purdum, the Pleasant Plains School. The first Sunday School classes were held here, before the Mt. View Church was built. The house which was built on the site was one-and-a-half stories and was constructed in the early twentieth century. The house had several additions and has been covered with siding. William Haller and Lucy Poole King lived here in 1920's and 1930's. The White family lived here in the late 1930's, followed by Hal and Vera Crawford. The Phalens lived here subsequently.

30. White-Smith-Haines Farm

William Alfred Smith purchased 100 acres of rolling farm land in 1877 from George C. White. The Smiths lived in the old log house until the two-story three bay by one bay frame house was built in 1887. It has two center chimneys and eight rooms. The steeply pitched center gable has an arched window and returned corners and is typical of late nineteenth century architecture. The roof is covered in raised seam metal and the wooden porch has turned posts with a balustrade runs the length of the porch. William Smith was a tabacco farmer, store keeper and post master. Eliza Ann Young Smith was the local mid-wife and nurse. The bank barn is 36' by 30' and the other outbuildings include the chicken house, corncrib and smoke house. Following the death of "Al" Smith, Eliza rented rooms to Jesse and Jane Haines and Raymond and Stella Runkles Allnutt. In 1937 Walter Edward Haines, Jr., Eliza's grandson, came to live here with his wife Ruth Estelle Watkins Haines. Mr. Haines lives here presently.

31. Anderson - Thomas House

This home is located on Price's Distillery Road near the intersection of Burnt Hill Road. In the 1920's Tom and Bessie Anderson lived here with their children: Walter, Melvin, Theodore, Lansdale and Lucille. It is now owned and occupied by John 'Ding' Thomas and his family. One of his sons now owns the home across the street with was previously in the Hawkins family. Several other houses near the corner of Burnt Hill Road were destroyed by fire.

32. Brown House
Burnt Hill Road

Thomas E. Brown sold this property to Titus E. Brown in 1903 and the the two-story frame house dates to that time. It is three bays by one bay with a gable roof and center gable facade. The chimney is of brick and in the rear ell there is an additional chimney. The facade has an arched window in center gable. The roof of the front porch is supported by six turned bracketed posts. The house was built for Titus E. and Agnes Matilda Browning Brown. His brother Thurston 'Jack' Brown lived here with them. After Agnes died Titus married Roberta Eveline Watkins Burdette and moved to Browningsville. They sold it to Frank and Foley Barrow who lived here with their daughters until the mid-1950's. The Blankenships lived here and presently Tony Mossburg lives here. The facade has been remodeled with stone.

33. Luhn-Denu House

This was a log house built by Ellsworth McCullough Smith. His son Willard 'Bill' Smith was born here before the family moved to Purdum before 1920. The house was sold to Daniel Price who sold it to Lawrence W. and Clara Belle Luhn in 1936. They had additions put on each side and the house was wired for electricity at this time. The electrician verified that the original house was built of logs. Presently it is a one-and-a-half story frame house, four bay by three bays, with dormers in the hipped roof. The outbuildings have stone foundations and the chicken house is particularly handsome. The property was conveyed to their son, Ray Luhn, who sold it to the Melvin and Patricia Denu in 1977. Across the street from this house was the home of William R. Davis, Sr. and Jessie Watkins Davis. It is no longer standing.

34. John Middleton King Farm

The foundation of the old house is visible to the left of the bank barn. From Burnt Hill Road looking at the remaining outbuildings one has a picturesque view of Sugarloaf Mountain above the tree line. The foundation of the bank barn is stone. The house was built for John Middleton King and his wife Amy Catherine Brewer, whom he married in 1853. He was a son of Middleton King and Mahala E. Summers King. The property is presently owned by Chester Leishear.

35. Earl King Farm

This farm was parceled from "Trouble Enough". The property was purchased by Pearl Clark King and Alice E. Price King who were married in 1902. The barn burned and was rebuilt c. 1916. Their son, Earl Virginia King, and his wife Mildred Frances Brown King were the subsequent owners. They raised their family here and farmed. Presently Dr. Tom Hartsock raises goats here. The stone foundation of the barn is a spectacular example of local masonry.

36. Burdette House

The left section of this dwelling is of hand hewn log and was built by John Edwin Burditt c. 1858 after he married Mary Ellen Watkins. This section was three bays by one bay and had a stone chimney and hearth. There was a loft overhead and curved steps with a closet underneath were built in the corner. The interior was paneled below the chair rail and at one time was painted salmon. The roof is corrugated metal and the chimney was replaced with an interior brick chimney c. 1895 when the second section was added. Willie Hampton Burdette and his wife Jennie E. Pugh farmed and raised their family here. Willie was a son of John and Mary Burditt, an early spelling of the present form of the name. The second section is two bays by one bay with two floors. The interior walls were plastered and the exterior of the home was covered with siding. When Willie and Jennie moved to Browningsvlle their son, Milton W. Burdette, was the third generation to live here. He was also a lay preacher. He married Mary Rebecca Watkins and later sold the property and moved to Browningsville. The house was then used to store hay.

37. King - Jamison House

This two-story three bay by one bay frame house was at one time the home of Pearl Clark King. On June 6, 1913 Ernest King sold the property to Eugene Angleo Jamison. The house has a gable roof and center gable facade and a center brick chimney. The facade has a full-length porch with roof supported by bracketed turned posts. The roof and porch roof are of corrugated metal. A rear addition has been constructed. Eugene and his wife, Exie Purdum Jamison, lived here with their children Estelle, Edith, Claudia and Purdum. Clint Wachter and his wife lived here. They were killed in an accident near Baltimore and Chester Leishear purchased the property.

38. Lawson House

The original section of this house was the portion on the left, between the brick chimneys. The house was originally of log construction, but was weatherboarded and a two-story addition was built and a section of the porch was enclosed. James Draper Lawson received this land in the late 18th century and his son Gabriel Lewis Duvall Lawson married Ann Jeanette Moxley c. 1842. They farmed and raised their family here. Their children were Richard H., Ann, Josiah Wolfe, Caleb "Crit", Mary, Emma and Sarah Lawson. Richard and "Crit" Lawson farmed here and later sold the property to Wilbur Luhn. The foundation of the house is located beside a stream. Although not visible in the photograph, the farm had a picturesque windmill.

39. Day House

This two-story three bay by two bay frame house was built for Frank Day c. 1910. It has a gable roof with a center gable facade, a wrap around porch with turned, bracketed posts and two brick chimneys. The house has had several additions. The house was purchased by Edward L. and Inez Burdette and sold to Chester and Ethel Leishear.

## The History of Browningsville

Browningsville was named for the Browning family who were among the early settlers of this vicinity. Located at the intersection of Bethesda Church Road and Clarksburg Road, it is one of the villages that developed in the Clarksburg district during the middle part of the nineteenth century. Browningsville grew from the grist mill and saw mill surrounded by farms on gently rolling hills. In 1870 Christian and David Bear were blacksmiths, William Fleming was a shoemaker, Jonathan Jacobs and John L. Snyder were coachmakers, William T. Turner and George W. Moxley were millers and Belt M. Norwood was a carpenter.

By 1866, Samuel Hobbs operated a general merchandise store which offered dry goods, groceries, hardware, boots, shoes, drugs and notions. Reuben Engle also operated a store. Jonathan Jacobs operated the blacksmith and wheel wright shop. David Henry King operated a shoe shop. In 1881 the merchants were S. M. Benton & Brother, Reuben Engle and Samuel Hobbs, who was also the postmaster. Browning and Jacobs carriage making business was also located at the intersection. The road now called Clarksburg Road was at one time called Turner's Mill Road and later, Gladhill Road. The road plat for Barnes Road was also drawn in 1881. It remains the same today as it appeared at that time. Browningsville had it's own library from 1880 - 1915 and some books are still marked "Browningsville Literary Society". Electricity became available to area residents in the late 1920's and party-line telephone service was available in the 1930's.

## Postmasters of Browningsville

| | |
|---|---|
| Richard H. Williams | March 10, 1832 |
| Samuel Hobbs | September 1, 1879 |
| William H. Broadhurst | April 27, 1891 |
| Samuel Hobbs | January 25, 1899 |
| William Broadhurst | July 31, 1899 |

Mail service discontinued, sent to Monrovia November 14, 1899

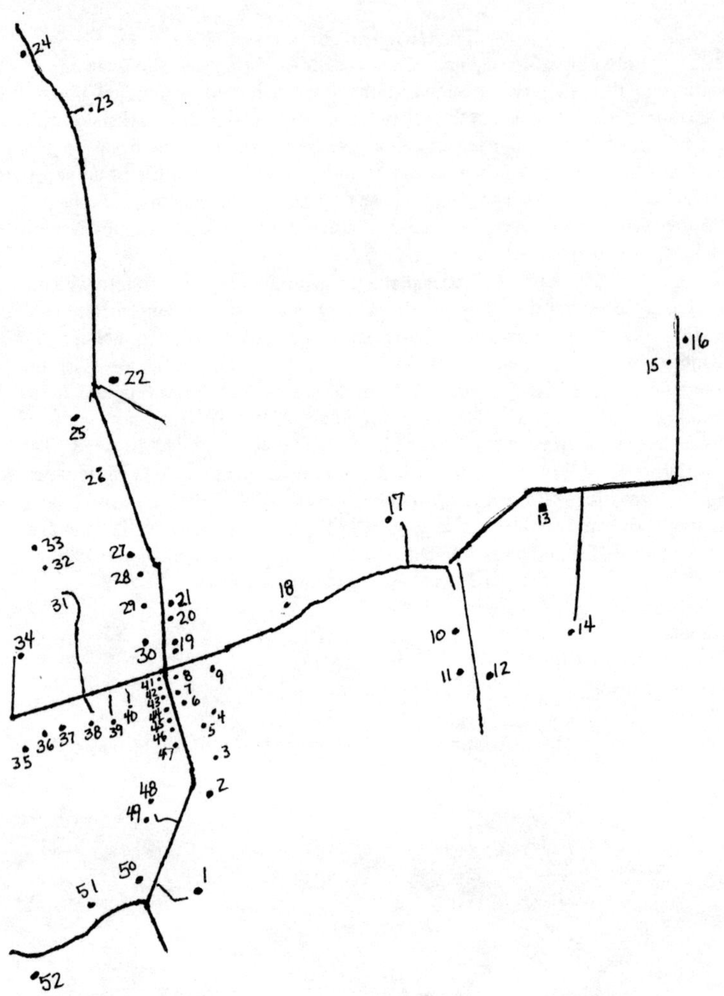


**Map of Browningsville**

The Browningsville Band was organized by William A. Walker in 1884 with 20 members. The band has played at church picnics, fairs, parades and other concerts. Their signature piece is "And the Band Played On." The band practiced every Friday evening in the Browningsville Hall January through June. They are non-profit, self-supporting and completely volunteer group. Fees for their performances pay for uniforms, instrument repair, hall rental and other upkeep. Raymond F. Day and Dwight Talmadge Walker were with the band for over 50 years. Mr. Walker was a son of the founder.

Photograph of 1906 band members front (left to right): Lewis E. Purdum, A. W. Lawson, Emory Purdum, Josie Burdette, James V. Baker, William L. Purdum. Middle: V. D. Watkins, James S. Day, Grant Watkins, Rufus E. Baker, Granville Mullinix, Carl Purdum, Tobias Watkins. Back: Reese Watkins, J. R. Lewis, Lester Moxley, William A. Walker, Garrison Moxley, Ernest Moxley, Ezra Brandenburg.

## Houses and Building in Browningsville

1. Watkins House

This property was part of the Samuel B. Watkins farm, which was sold following his death in 1885. His grandson Maurice Watkins purchased this parcel and the house was built c. 1894. Maurice Watkins and his wife Martha Rebecca King Watkins raised their family here, and he farmed the land. Their son, William Maurice Watkins, married Fannie Wagner McEflresh and lived here subsequently. The house is a two-story three bay Victorian-style with a gable roof and a center gable. The gable facade has a single arch window and the full-length front porch was replaced by the present portico in 1950's. The property was sold to Mr. Wheatley who sold it to Walter Smith. In the 1960's the property was sold to the late Colonel Edward Wilson and Rita Wilson.

2. Maurice Snyder House

This Victorian-style frame house was built in 1899 Maurice M. and Edith E. Purdum Snyder. The residence is a two-story three bay with a gabled roof covered in corrigated metal. The front porch has a hipped roof supported by ornately bracketed turned posts. The rear ell is two-story two bay and the exterior of the house is covered in German siding. Maurice was a millwright and he grew tobacco here. His father John L. Snyder immigrated from Germany and was a coachmaker and later a huckster.

3. Browningsville Schoolhouse

After the older Browningsville School burned, the community requested $500 to build a new school. The one acre property was purchased from John E. and Mary Warfield for $75. The single-story frame building with tongue in groove siding, and a raised seam metal roof, was constructed in 1899. The principal at that time was Willis B. Burdette. The recessed entrance had a transome light above the door. The Trustees were W. H. Broadhurst, Miel E. Linthicum, and Joseph McKendree Burdette. In 1900 the teachers were Helen Augusta Day and Fidelia S. Walker. When Franklin S. Gladhill came as principal in 1906 the building received an addition. The tower and east room of the school were constructed and between the two main rooms was a large sliding door that could be retracted for use as a larger room. Flora Watkins and Maude Ashton also taught here. The community requested that high school courses be offered at the school in 1923 by an additional teacher, or that the county provide transportation to the high school. The teacher in 1925-1926 was Elsie Green. There was a baseball field in back, near the privy. Moody Burdette helped James W. Day replaced the glass panels several times after baseballs broke some of the windows. In June of 1932 the school closed it's door and the students were transported to Damascus. The building was sold for $90 to Maurice Snyder on July 13, 1933. The bell is on display in the museum of Bernard "Buck" Gladhill. It once was housed in the bell tower on the north side of the school in an open bell cote.

Class of 1911 Front: Raymond King, Howard Watkins, Purdum Snyder, Obey Beall, Wilford Kidwell, Marshall Buxton, Harold Lydard. 2nd: Henry King, Melvin King, Ralph Layton, Tom Lydard, Joseph Day, Filmore Lewis, Wellington Beall, Miel Linthicum, Willie Watkins, Wilson Clay, Gilbert Broadhurst. 3rd: Fannie McElfresh, Erica Purdum, Joyce Purdum, Mary Poole, Betty Kidwell, Louise Baker, Mary Watkins, Rose Baker, Lettie Lydard, Flora Watkins, Mary Baker, Fernie Watkins, Gladys Claggett, Maude Ashton. 4th: Franklin S. Gladhill, Principal, Lansdale Burdette, Otis Watkins, Wilson Beall, Ethel Smith, Rhodie Clay, Roberta Watkins, Agnes Broadhurst. 5th: Rosie Beall, Iva Watkins, Virgie Day, Ethel Buxton, Ethel Linthicum, Winnie Watkins, Linda Broadhurst, Percy Claggett.

Browningsville students c. 1920

Class of 1926 Front: Virginia Burdette, Marie Beall, Gertrude Disney, Louise Barnes, Leroy Sherman, Evelyn Walker, Second: Edwin Linthicum, Madeline Bennett, Alma Burdette, Franklin Weller, Georgia Gladhill, Marion Barnes, 3rd: Stewart Walker, Dorothy Barnes, Edna Shipley, Harold Watkins, Lester Payne, Elsie Snyder, 4th: Lillian Gladhill, Beatrice Cutsail, Phyllis Shipley, Margaret Disney, Back: Marvin Burdette, Mabel Pearson, and Elsie Green, teacher.

4. Grimes House

Samuel L. Shipley built this residence for William H. Grimes and his wife of one year, Mary "Mollie" Exeline Mullinix Grimes. Built in 1904 it was a rural vernacular style two-story frame dwelling with a gable roof and center gable. Mary Browning Williams lived here for many years and raised here four sons here. The property was purchased in 1971 by the present owner Bill Thom. He had some remodeling done at which time the rear porch was enclosed to make a sun room. Bill and Susan Thom live here at the present time.

5. Burdette-Shipley-Myers House

On this site before the house was built stood the store of Reuben Engle who sold the building to William Grimes, when he moved from Hyattstown to operate a cobbler shop. A house was built on the site of the shop by Samuel L. Shipley for his son John W. who married Cora M. Sheckles Shipley in 1915. The house burned down and was rebuilt to the original specifications. This second dwelling is three bays by one bay with a corrigated metal gabled roof. The wooden shed roof porch runs the length of the facade and is supported by ornately bracketed turned posts with a balustrade. The house has retained most of it's original features, making it an excellent example of the architecture of the Victorian period. The brick chimney is in the rear and the exterior is covered with narrow German siding. Their children were: Edna Shipley Riggleman, Mazie Gue, Thelma Johnson and Kenneth Shipley who lived here before the house was sold to Marian Myers in 1982.

6. Burdette Bungalow

This property was part of the land purchased by Willie H. Burdette after he sold his farm between King's Valley and Purdum. In 1936 he sold this quarter acre to his son Milton W. Burdette, who built this house. The house is one-story and rectangular in shape, being a modified bungalow style structure. It is three bay by three bay and of frame construction. The gabled roof extends to form a front porch supported by Doric columns with a balustrade. Milton and Mary Rebecca Watkins Burdette had resided across the street with his parents briefly before the house was built.

7. Jonathan Jacobs House

Jonathan Jacobs and his wife, Mary Manzella Brandenburg Jacobs, were married in 1867 and lived here. Jacob, and his son William, operated a blacksmith and wheelwright shop on the corner of the intersection. The residence is two-story three bay by one bay frame with a gabled roof. The rear ell is two-story one bay deep with a gabled roof. The front porch runs the length of the facade and it's roof is supported by ornately bracketed turned posts. The subsequent owner was Moody McComas Burdette who operated the store across the road which is no longer standing. Mrs. Ellen Grace Kidwell Burdette continued to live here after Moody Burdette died in 1945. The Shry family and Anthony Smith lived here. Presently Ben Melton and family own the house and reside here.

8. Jacob's Blacksmith and Wheelwright Shop

The corner of Bethesda Church Road and Clarksburg Road was the site of a two-story building which was used for a blacksmith and wheelwright shop and carriage shop on the second floor. Inside, buggies and wagons were built and finished on the second floor and rolled down a ramp on wheels made in the blacksmith shop. The wagon body pictured below was made by Jonathan and his son William T. Jacobs at this location and the side reads: "J. Jacobs and Son Builders, Browningsville, Md." The wagon remains are in the collection of Bernard "Buck" Gladhill. Jonathan Jacobs patented a wagon wheel brake called "Jacob's Rubber". The second floor of the shop was also the site of templars meetings and other gatherings.

9. site of old Browningsville School

In 1882, after Joseph Hager sold the lot to the Montgomery County School Board, a public school was built on this site. For the fifteen years prior to this, students had walked to the Lighthill School. The Browningsville School, which was school #3 in Election District #2, burned in December of 1896. Between January of 1897 and September of 1899 the students attended the Lewisdale school while the new school was under construction. The school site is off Bethesda Church Road.

10. Burdette Farm

This property off Purdum Road was once the farm of Benjamin and Mary Burdett. The first log house on the farm was built c. 1789. The older one-and-a-half-story section of this house was built of logs and the addition has two-stories. The brick chimney is between the two sections of the house which was built for James William and Cassandra Elizabeth Purdum Burdette. The bank barn was located across the road. There is a family cemetery in the field. Presently the property is owned by Chester Leishear.

11. Dorsey Day House

This was the Dorsey Waters Day and Prudence Virginia Burdette Day house. It was built of chestnut logs, and when Chester Leishear decided to have it torn down, it wouldn't budge, so he burned the house down. The older section was of log and was one-and-a-half-stories which had three bays, a central door-way with flanking windows. The other section was two-story with a two bay facade, with the chimney between the two sections, which were both on a stone foundation. The house had a kitchen wing, with an external stone fireplace with a brick stack. The house had been sheathed with clapboard siding.

12. James Willard Day House

The rear section of this residence was a log house with a central brick chimney. Set high on a hill, one can see the Bethesda United Methodist Church and much of the surrounding area from the front yard. The house has been in the family for several generations. James Willard and Edna M. Beall Day live here presently. The house faces Purdum Road.

13. Beall's Grove Camp Meeting

Methodist minister Fred Barnes and Evangelist J. R. Parker began holding camp meetings here in a tent in a grove of trees in 1931. The property was provided by Will and Cassandra Burdette Beall. The Beall Memorial Tabernacle was built in 1935 by an association of local layman. In 1962 the name Damascus Camp Meeting was adopted. The property is now owned by the Weslyan Church and there are 47 cabins, a chapel, girls and boys dormitories, trailer hook-ups, youth pavillion and recreational facilities on 12 acres of land. The dining hall was converted into a sanctuary for the Damascus Weslyan Church and the present pastor is Rev. Jerry S. Beall. Interdenominational camp is held annually in the summer.

14. Glaze Cabin

William T. and Sarah Ann McElfresh Glaze built this log house c. 1878 after buying the property from James W. Burdett. Originally it was a one-and-a-half story structure with a central hall and chimney. The logs were laid up with inverted V-notching. The interior walls were finished in a lap and plaster. The kitchen had a small interior chimney for the stove. Later the dwelling was covered in weatherboard siding. There was also a family cemetery here with slate markers. Ellwood and Mary Mullinix Franklin lived here and then Joseph Arthur Hurley purchased the property from Basil Russell and Bertie May King Glaze on March 25, 1926 and later married Esther Mae Thompson, who lived here for several years. In the 1940's Upton and Bernard Gladhill purchased the property to farm. At that time the cemetery markers were removed.

15. Dutrow Farm

Milton Boyer sold this farm to Delaney Brown. It had been in the Boyer family for many years. Lynda Pearl Brown married Mertlen Long Dutrow and lived in the older house until it burned in 1937. The present house was built in 1938 in 28 days by Bill Hawse. While the new house was under construction, the two chicken houses were joined and the family lived there. Merhle Eugene Dutrow purchased the property and lives here presently. A cemetery on the property is the resting place of Dr. George Milton Boyer's mother, Elizabeth W. Purdum Boyer.

16. Warthen Farm

This two-story frame house is three bay by two bays with two brick end chimneys. The gable roof has returned cornices. The roof of the front porch is supprted by square posts and a small side porch has been added. It was previously the farm of Gurney Warthen and presently the Powers live here.

17. Parson Day Farm

James Day purchased 153 acres which were part of "Solomon's Roguery," part of "Flaggpatch" and part of "Resolution" c. 1819. The property was sold after the death of his widow and subsequently this property is listed as the Louisa Day Baker farm in 1878. The house burned twice, and there was a family cemetery here, which was kept up by the family until the permit was not renewed, at which time it was plowed under to farm. The present house has been expanded, but it originally had two-stories and three bays and a center gable. The farm was operated as a dairy farm Edward and Marvin Burdette. It is presently a horse farm and riding school.

18. Lawson-Byrne House

William L. Lawson married Annie E. Lawson and purchased this property on March 27, 1878 from Luther M. Browning. He farmed here on Bethesda Church Road until 1898. The house had two-stories and was five bays by two bays. The original section had a one-story porch with the roof supported by bracketed posts with scalloped barge boards along the roof line. A one-story wing extended from the main house. In the photograph some of the clapboard siding is visible under the asbestos siding. The house was later owned by James N. Byrne, a Union veteran of the Civil War. The property was purchased by Edward Lewis and Inez Thomas Burdette who rented it to Mary Browning Williams. She kept the house in good condition, but after she moved to the Grimes house on Clarksburg Road subsequent tenants did not. One can still see the pile of desbris left from the old house. The remains of the old kitchen building can still be located.

19. Four log houses

Luther Browning purchased land from James Day in 1836 and built four log dwellings. At one time, Joseph Burdett lived in a house which was located on the corner. In 1854 Mr. Keller was living at this location. An 1884 mortgage mentions three of the structures and their present occupants: Eli J. Beall, William Bolton and Littleton M. Cuslett. The property was conveyed to Jonathan Browning in 1891. The houses remained in the Browning family until 1903 when they were sold for $850 to George Washington Cutsail. Sarah Cutsail, his widow, left the house pictured below to her sister Catherine Watkins, who retained possesion into the 1940's. When Esther Mae Thompson Hurley moved here the kitchen had been added. The log exterior was covered with faux brick asbestos siding while she resided here. James "Bill" and Margaret Hawes have lived since c. 1955. Next door was another log house which functioned as a creamery until 1918. During the 1920's Ed and Annie Sheckles Shipley lived there followed by Frank Williams and his family. The structure was gone by 1945.

20. Housen House

In October, 1836 James Day conveyed 17 1/2 acres to Luther Browning for $425. These log homes were probably built by or for Luther M. Browning, and then rented to various tenants. George Housen lived here in the 1880's. The house was later sheathed with clapboard siding. The rear addition was completed in the 1940's when Lew Gladhill owned the house. Kate Watkins, and her sister Martha shared this house for several years. Grace Ecker and her son live here presently.

21. Burdette House

This was part of the land conveyed to Luther Browning in 1836. This is the fourth of the log dwellings built here before 1878. The frame two-story house was constructed around the log section with three bays by two bays and a rear ell. The gabled roof was covered with composition shingles and the rear addition has an exterior brick chimney. Millard Burdette and family lived here, followed by his son, Allen Burdette. Further up the road, and up a lane was the Charles W. Browning house. It was a two-story three bay by two bay frame house the a gable roof and exterior brick chimney. Charles Browning taught at the Lighthill School in 1868 and married Emily Jennie Hodges of Comus in 1871. Following her death in 1872, he married Harriet Ann Watkins. Mr. Browning died in 1894. Millard Burdette, Sr., later lived in this house, which has been gone for many years. Still further up the road was the shoe shop and house which David Henry King lived in. The house was destroyed by fire in 1974.

22. William Boyer Farm

This was one of the houses on the Boyer farm. Colvin Hughsie McElfresh, Sr., purchased the property in 1901 from William Boyer. In 1912 Colvin H. McElfresh, Jr. purchased the land and sold it Ira McElfresh in 1922. The house is an American four-square with a dormer in the facade. The porch has been partially enclosed. The barn has a stone foundation and is in excellent condition. The Gladhills owned this property at one time.

23. Baker-Riggs-Luther House

This house was built in several sections. The section on the right was a log structure built by the Bakers. The second section was added, having three bays and both have been covered with aluminum siding. The full-length porch has a shed roof supported by six columns on brick piers. The Lester Riggs family lived here, followed by Dr. Luther, who resides here presently.

24. Boyer Farm

The Boyer farm was located on Clarksburg Road. The house was a two-story frame dwelling and had a three bay facade. The gable roof had a center gable with an arched window. Over the full-length front porch was a balcony with a balustrade. Two interior brick chimneys provided heat for the house. As of the 1990's the house was no longer standing.

25. Buxton House

Marshall and Lillian Buxton raised foster children and farmed here. The home is two-story frame house with a three bay facade. The gable roof has a center gable and returned cornices. The center gable and end gables have arched windows. The front porch roof is supported by squared posts on piers. The two-story ell has a side porch which has partially been enclosed. The field is rented and sheep graze here. On occasion one can watch boarder collies being trained in the fields.

26. Jefferson Day Farm

The original house was of log construction with an external chimney. It was built for Jefferson Day, son of James Day, after he married Mary Ann Warfield c. 1835. Mr. Day was a farmer and Methodist Protestant minister. He died in 1863 and on the 1879 Montgomery County Atlas Mary Ann Day is shown as the owner of the property. The house was later covered with siding and a raised seam metal roof was added. The front porch ran the length of the facade and the roof was supported by four posts. The foundation was of stone, and the house has been gone since the late 1970's.

27. Browningsville Mill

James Day built the mill on the Bennett's Creek c. 1804. He sold the grain mill and the property in 1818 to Eli Brashears for five hundred dollars. John Boyer was the subsequent miller from 1839 to 1854. William T. Turner was the miller from 1869 until 1903. William and Belle Broadhurst operated the mill for awhile, as did the Burdettes. Monroe Turner was the miller when the barn caught fire in 1906 and the fire spread to the mill. Franklin S. Gladhill purchased the property and rebuilt the mill in 1908. The Gladhills were the last to operate the Browningsville mill before it was torn down. The water crossed Clarksburg Road in an over head trough built high above the road until it was graded and paved; at which time the race went under the road.

28. James Day House

In 1802 Peter Boyer and James Day purchased "Flaggpatch" and "Solomon's Roguery" and the in 1803 they traded section of each tract. Boyer sold 152 acres of the to James Day for five shillings and 160 acres of land. Day built the mill on the Bennett's Creek and a small log dwelling. He sold the grain mill and property in 1818 to Eli Brashears for five hundred dollars. John Boyer was the subsequent owner from 1839 until 1854. In 1869 William T. Turner purchased the mill property. The addition probably was built during this time. The mill burned, but was rebuilt on the same foundation. Franklin S. Gladhill owned the mill and lived here beginning in 1908. Seven of the eight Gladhill children were born here. The orginal log section of the house is now the rear ell with an exerior brick chimney. The addition is a five bay frame two story dwelling. Georgia Gladhill Cline lived here and remodeled the house. Mr. and Mrs. Stewart Walker purchased the property and sold it to the Lindburg's in the late 1970's. The Eustice family purchased it subsequently.

29. Layton House

Between the store and the Day house was the home of Sadie Layton who was a dressmaker. She did alterations for local people and sewed dresses and beaded gowns for a lady from New York. She also made wedding gowns for ladies in the area. Between this house and the corner was the Hobb's Store, which opened in the mid-1860's and was at one time also the post office. A millinery shop was located in the back of the store. Mr. Hobb's sons-in-law also were merchants here: Fletcher A. Day and John L. Walker. By 1900 the Mr. Hobbs retired and Mr. Walker was the owner. Some entries from the store ledger are included on the following page.

Hobbs' Store Ledger

The set of store ledgers dates from the mid-1860's. Below are some entries from 1910.

| | | |
|---|---|---|
| Mrs. David King | 1 pound of salt | .05 |
| | 2 pair of hose for Dave | .30 |
| | 1 pair of gloves for Dave | .10 |
| | 3 yards of shirting | .30 |
| | credit for work | $2.00 |
| Miel Linthicum | 3 pounds of dynamite | .54 |
| | 12 dozen blasting caps | .12 |
| | 21 feet of fuse | .77 |
| | 10 pounds of staples | .60 |
| | paid by check | |
| William L. Purdum | 5 cloves cinnamon | .05 |
| | 1/2 pound Borax | .08 |
| | lamp chimney | .06 |
| | 5 gallons of coal oil | .63 |
| | 16 pounds of early clover seed | $3.12 |
| | 5 pounds of sugar | .28 |
| Samuel Shipley | 75 pounds of Timothy seed | $4.88 |
| Mrs. Samuel Shipley | 10 yards of calico | .60 |
| | 1 yard of gingham | .07 |
| Bradley Watkins | 10 pounds of bacon | $1.00 |
| | x-ray backing | .05 |
| | package of coffee | .17 |
| | 3 spools of cotton | .15 |
| | 1/2 pound dried peaches | .05 |
| | 1 bar sweetheart soap | .05 |
| | 1 bottle vaseline | .05 |
| | 1 chocolate cake | .18 |
| | 2 lamp wicks | .02 |

30. Browningsville Hall

The Browningsville Hall was built in 1921 of frame construction by local citizens. It is six bays long and three bays wide. The lot was conveyed by John L. and Harriet E. Hobbs Walker and Elizabeth Cutsail in January, 1922 to a board of trustees for a hall for the Bethesda Methodist Episcopal Church. The International Order of Good Templars lodge #184 held their meetings here. The Browningsville Band practiced here, and also church suppers, MYF meetings, receptions, Sunday School picnics, Y. M. C. A. and Epworth League meetings have been held here over the years. It had a stage up front for plays, programs, etc. It is owned and maintained by the Walker family.

31. Mendelssohn Terrace

The elegant two-story frame house was built by John Mount in 1880 for George Washington Wesley and Rachel Browning Purdum Walker. It was the first house in the area built with indoor plumbing. The house was named "Mendelssohn" for his daughter's favorite composer, and the farm is called Mendelssohn Terrace. The house features a central hall with flanking parlors, and an oval staircase which is open to the third floor. George studied under Methodist hymn writer Lowell Mason in Florida, New York while he was in college. He farmed, taught music lessons, played the organ, ran singing schools, and sold Miller organs to local families and churches in the area. The farm was purchased by his son, John Lewis E. Walker and wife Harriet Ann Eugenia Hobbs Walker. The Walkers operated a threshing business, a saw mill, well-drilling, and offered stud services. Brothers Eugene and Gwynn Walker inherited the farm in the 1920's. In 1952 Stewart and his wife, Eunice Burdette Walker, purchased the farm from Eugene's heirs. Mrs. Walker owns the farm presently. Her sons, Stewart Eugene, Jr. and Darryl Walker, live on and operate the dairy farm. The bank barn dates to the 1840's.

Walker Saw Mill

John L. E Walker and King Bruno

32. Boyer Home

Peter Boyer and Anna Mary Musseter Boyer purchased 140 acres of "Henry and Elizabeth Enlarged" in 1795, and resided in the log house which was built c. 1760. The dwelling had an external stone chimney and is pictured below c. 1880. Mr. Boyer grew tobacco and wormweed. His son, Peter Boyer, Jr., also farmed here, and he and his wife Catherine may have lived here following his father's death in 1805. The site of the cabin is part of the Walker farm, Mendelssohn Terrace.

33. George B. Walker House

The first section of the cabin was built across from the cabin on the preceding page. It may have been the home of Peter Boyer and Anna Mary Musseter Boyer or Peter Boyer, Jr., and Catherine Boyer. George Bryan Walker married Margaret Boyer c. 1822 and purchased 142 acres from Peter and Catherine Boyer in 1830. The second section of the house was built c. 1840. Their son, George Washington Wesley Walker was raised here, and in 1858 married Rachel Browning Purdum. During the Civil War a soldier was cared for here, but died. There is a family cemetery on the property in which the soldier is buried, as well as the Boyers and three of the Walker family members.

34. Purdum Farm

John Lewis Purdum farmed here and by 1900 Miel E. Linthicum lived here. The farm was conveyed to his son Purdum Linthicum who sold it to Raymond and Talmadge Bennett in the 1940's. After a land trade, Raymond Bennett became the sole owner. He sold the farm to Millard Burdette, Jr., and Madeline Bennett Burdette, but the house is now gone. It was a two-story three bay farm house with a center gable. The front porch ran the length of the facade and the porch roof was supported by four posts. The house was heated by two brick interior end chimneys. A large bank barn had picturesque air vents in the roof. Several outbuildings remain and a sub-division is now behind the farm.

35. Day-Snyder House

In 1854 this was the property of William Burdette. The land was sold to Titus Granville Day and his bride Laura Dorcas Watkins Day. The house was built for them c. 1886. She was a daughter of Samuel B. Watkins, whose land had just been parcelled at this time. Victorian two-story frame three bay house with central chimneys, gable roof, center gable with returned corners and arched window in the gable. The front porch roof is supported by bracketed turned posts with a balustrade. The front door has sidelights and a turret has been added to the side. Mr. Day died in 1931, and Mrs. Day died in 1940. Forrest and Sarah Snyder purchased the house which was sold to the Wetsteins and then to Andrew and RoseAnn Armes.

Browningsville's Methodist Church was named Bethesda from a text in John 5 meaning a house of mercy. It was the name of a place of miraculous healing—the pool of Bethesda. John and Julianna Boyer Bear sold one acre to the Trustees for one cent on June 8, 1808. The Trustees were: James Day, Hezekiah Summers, John Dillworth, Ephraim Etchison, Frederick Adamson and Adam Boyer. James Day was active in the church, preaching sermons and was liscensed to exhort. The first church was of log construction and was referred to as "Jimmy Day's Meeting House." During the Civil War a wounded soldier was brought to the church.

In 1843 Sunday School classes began. Some of the past Superintendents have been: Caleb Crittendon Lawson, James W. Burdette, Samuel Hobbs, Caleb Joshua Burdette, Miel Linthicum, Charles Housen, Filmore Beall, Eugene S. Walker, Milton Burdette, Charlie Burdette, Esther Beall, Lansdale Burdette, Harold Watkins, Lindy Beall, Alfred Freysz, Fred Beall and Joan Stanley. Among the Secretaries have been Belle Broadhurst and Rudell Beall.

The Act of Incorporation was dated November 24, 1854. The cemetery land was purchased from John D. Purdum in 1891. In 1927 an additional acre was donated by Meil and Mary Linthicum and another acre in 1950 from Millard and Madeline Burdette. The perpetual care fund was supervised by Stewart E. Walker and presently by Harold Bennett.

In 1871 a cornerstone was laid for the Bethesda Methodist Church. This church was of frame construction and was built by James R. Mount. The building committee consisted of James W. Burdette, Luther M. Browning, George W. Walker, Samuel Hobbs, William T. Turner, Basil Beall, Joseph S. Watkins, Caleb J. Burdette and Rufus K. Day.

In 1907 the church pictured on the following page was built. The end of each roof section was gabled and three had a round windows, while the fourth had three arched windows. The bell tower was added with a bell donated by George W. Walker. Later the church was covered in aluminum siding. Due to a termite infestation this building was burned after the stained glass windows, chancel, bell and other items were removed to the new church complex in 1978. The burning was video taped by the historical society.

In 1965 five additional acres were purchased from Millard and Madeline Burdette for the present church complex which includes the church, ballfield and pavillion. The present church complex opened in 1978, and was dedicated on June 19, 1988. The church was consecrated by Bishop James K. Matthews. The pulpit and chairs from the 1871 church building are being used in the new sanctuary. The pastors since 1868 have been:

| | |
|---|---|
| James D. Still | 1868-70 |
| Harrison McNemar | 1871-74, J. S. M. Haslip, assistant |
| T. Marshall West | 1874-77 |
| Emory Buhrman | 1877-80 |
| Randolph Richardson Murphy | 1880-83 |
| W. R. Gwinn | 1883-86, A. H. Thompson, assistant |
| Thomas J. Cross | 1886-90, A. H. Thompson, assistant |
| J. R. Pardew | 1890-92 |
| W. F. Roberts | 1892-94 |
| J. W. Steele | 1894-96 |
| William Harris | 1896-99 |
| E. Elmer Marshall | 1899-1902 |
| Caleb M. Yost | 1902-11 |
| Thomas S. Davis | 1911-16 |
| Walter S. Jones | 1916-17 |
| Frank Y. Jaggers | 1917-20 |
| Wallace M. Brashears | 1920-26 |
| W. E. Nelson | 1926-30 |
| Fred R. Barnes | 1930-35 |
| Hartwell F. Chandler | 1935-40 |
| Ira W. Shindle | 1940-42 |
| W. D. Eye | 1942-45 |
| E. Kyle Sawyers | 1945-47 |
| Don E. Griffin | 1947-53 |
| Ernest L. Harrison | 1953-56 |
| William T. Miller | 1956-58 |
| Hayden L. Sparks | 1958-63 |
| Richard C. Johnson | 1963-68 |
| James E. Chance | 1968-79 |
| Michael Leftwich | 1980-85 |

Bruce Hathorne 1985-88
Henry G. Butler 1988-

The memorial stained glass windows that were placed in the church during the 1907 renovations include: The physician's window—from fourteen area doctors solicited by Perepa Day; William T. and Keziah Turner; James Burdette, Casander Burdette, S. B. and Sara J. Watkins; the Lawson window; Browning window; Rufus K. and Ann P. Day; George B. Walker; Margaret Boyer Walker; Hobbs window; Linthicum window; Mr. and Mrs. Gabriel Lawson; Bethesda Sunday School window; and Nora M. Day. Other windows memorialize the Purdums, Rosabelle Walker, Jonathan and Mary M. Jacobs, Mr. and Mrs. Miel E. Linthicum, Mr. and Mrs. Caleb Crittendon Lawson and the International Order of Good Templars, Bethesda Lodge.

Other memorials include the chimes which were given in 1970 in memory of Lansdale Burdette who served as a Trustee for over 50 years. The offering plates were given by Mr. and Mrs. Glenwood D. King in memory of their parents. The electric candles were given by the family of Ethel Lawson in her memory. The pulpit Bible was donated in 1937.

The land for a parsonage was parceled from the Walker's property. In 1942 Eugene and Mary Walker and John Raymond Walker deeded land to the Montgomery Circuit for a residence for the preacher. The new parsonage was constructed on two additional acres from the Burdette family.

37. Bradley Watkins House

In 1854 this was the land of John L. Purdum. This two-story frame house was built c. 1919. It has a three bay facade, a center brick chimney, an end chimney and a two-story rear ell with two wings. The rear ell also has a brick chimney. This was the home of Sadie Layton Davis and her daughter Lois Lillian Davis until they moved to the house which was next to the present hall. In 1924 Bradley and Becky Watkins moved here from their farm in Lewisdale. Charles Hanford and Vivian Barnes Browning lived here and then sold the property to Harold Bennett in 1958. Roby Shipley rented the house in the early 1960's and the Elwood and Doris Furr stayed here until the early 1970's. In 1985 the house was sold to Thomas Reise. Robert and Pamela Bryce were the subsequent owners

38. Filmore Beall

The Filmore and Fannie Watkins Beall house is a two-story frame house with three bays and a gable roof with a central chimney. The front porch runs the length of the facade and is the roof is supported by bracketed turned posts. Their son, James Monroe Beall was born in 1903, and he was an infant when the house was built. The land for this farm was parceled from the Watkins farm.

39. Day House

This property was parceled from the Walker farm c. 1929 for Joseph Dorsey Day and Edith Weller Day, his wife. His daughter, Annie Laurie Day was born in the house and lives here presently. The house was built c. 1929 and is a two-story frame bungalow style house. The roof extends over the front porch to form the porch roof. There is a single dormer with three windows on the facade. Part of the front porch has been enclosed, and two columns on brick piers remain. The balustrade ends in front of the center doorway. The house sits on the crest of a hill with a field in front of it.

40. Eastbank

Eastbank was the home of John Lewis Everett Walker and his wife Harriet Ann Eugenia Hobbs Walker, and is thought to have been built c. 1885. The two-story frame house was three bays by one bay and was heated by a central chimney. The gable roof had a center facade gable with return cornices and an arched window in each gable. After 1924 the home was used as a tenant house until it was destroyed by fire in the 1940's or 1950's.

41. Burdette's Store

Moody Burdette operated the store that previously stood on the corner in Browningsville. The photograph below shows that the store was a single story frame building with two additions. There was also a filling station here in the 1930's. The family members on the porch beginning second from left are: Sadie Layton Davis, Moody Burdette, Ellen Kidwell Burdette, Irving Burdette, and Merle Burdette.

42. Housen's Store

George Housen operated the general store here in this two bay by four bay frame building which is on a stone foundation. Charlie Housen was the merchant here at the turn of the twentieth century. The property was purchased in 1959 by Otis L. and Byrd Emma Watkins. The Watkins ran a country store on the first floor and lived upstairs. Mrs. Watkins died in 1977 and it is now owned by Jerry Smith. The building has been covered with aluminum siding.

43. Beall House

The house that was here was built for Edward T. and Imogene Poole Beall prior to 1900. He was a local house painter. It was a frame two-story dwelling, three bays by one bay, and featured a center gabled roof covered with raised seam metal. The center entrance had two over two light sash windows on each side. The house had a center brick chimney and had been covered in asbestos shingles. The house had been significantly altered over the years. Obed and Virgie Beall were the last residents, and the house and lot were left the Bethesda United Methodist Church after their deaths. The property is now a parking lot with a garage which are used by Jerry Smith.

44. Broadhurst - Lawson House

This house was built for the Broadhurst family by Samuel L. Shipley, a stone mason and carpenter c. 1896. John P. Lawson purchased the property and lived here with his wife, Ida Elizabeth Ashton Lawson. John had operated a store in King's Valley before retiring in Browningsville. He died in 1915 and Mrs. Lawson died in 1934. The house was inherited by her niece, Mary Maude Ashton, who was a teacher at Kingsley. Miss Ashton came to Browningsville and taught for a few years, but later returned to Kingsley. Mr. Sanbower lived here and last family to live here was the Parks. Ths house is no longer standing. It had a two bay facade and a center brick chimney. The shed roof porch was supported by four turned posts. The houses in this area had no indoor plumbing and did not meet county codes for new owners.

45. Burdette-Larman House

Built c. 1900 in the rural vernacular style, this frame dwelling has been altered less than it's neighbors and is the best example of the style. The two-story, three-bay wide, one bay deep, with a raised seam metal roof. The center gable has an arched window and wooden shingles. The front porch has a hipped roof supported by bracketed turned posts. The house was built by Samuel Shipley. The exterior walls have been covered with German siding. The house was later sold to Willie Hampton Burdette, father of Milton Burdette, who lived here with his wife Mary Rebecca Watkins Burdette until they built the house across the road. Later, Mildred Larman lived here for many years.

46. Shipley House

This frame house was built by Samuel L. Shipley c. 1899. He and his wife, Mary Elizabeth Grimes Shipley, lived in Howard County prior to moving to Browningsville. They had eight children: Adeline Watkins, Edward, Walker, John, Frank, Violena King, Maurice and Zerah B. Beall. The house was two-stories with a three bay facade. The gabled roof was covered with raised seam metal and the gables had returned cornices. The house was heated by two interior brick end chimneys. A low hipped-roof wooden porch supported by bracketed turned posts and enclosed with screen, ran the length of the facade. Mary Elizabeth Grimes Shipley, daughter of William and Zeriah B. McElfresh Grimes of Hyattstown, died in 1928. Samuel Shipley, local builder and stone mason, died in 1948. Turner Keith resided here followed by John and Elsie Green. Subsequently Eddie and Ruth Grubb and his family were the last residents to live here. Zerah Belle Shipley Beall relates that these house were built from old tobacco barns.

47. Shipley-Franklin House

After the death of John R. Shipley, Mary Ellen Snowden Shipley had her son Samuel Shipley build this house for her c. 1900. Harry, Alonzo Shipley and sister Mary Shipley resided with their mother in this two-story frame house. The dwelling has a gabled roof and was built in a rural vernacular style. It is three bays across, one bay deep and has a front porch with cornices. The center chimney is brick and the exterior has been covered in asbestos shingles. Subsequent owners include Margaret Disney, daughter of Ida May Thomas Disney, and then Walter Haines sold the house to Elwood and Mary Mullinix Franklin. There was another house next to this one that has been gone for many years. It was owned by the Broadhurst's and sat very close to the creek. The Shipleys lived there while their house was under construction, and subsequently Talmadge and Libby Bennett lived there briefly. Their daughter Madeline Bennett was born there.

48. Smith House

This house was built by Samuel L. Shipley for Tony Smith and his wife Jenny Shipley Smith, who was Samuel's sister. The Smiths had three children: Ethel, Roy and Norman. When Jenny's brother Gassaway's wife died, Jenny and Tony raised their daughter, Phyllis Shipley. After the 1940's the property sold to the Nahr's who sold it to Forrest and Cora Fort. This is a two-story three bay by one bay frame house with gable roof, center gable facade with arched four pane window. The front porch has been enclosed and a wing has been added on the side.

49. Broadhurst House

Built for Samuel and Caroline C. Broadhurst by Samuel L. Shipley c. 1899. Samuel was a grain thrasher for area farms. The house has a steeply pitched gable on the right and both gables have an arched four pane window. The two-story frame house is the home of the Judy's Jamboree Nursery.

50. Watkins House

This property was part of Samuel B. Watkins land which was divided in after his death in 1885. After his grandson purchased this parcel, the hired hands lived in the then three or four room house. In 1925 the addition was constructed and the present T-shape was formed. Both sections have an interior brick chimney. Presently their son, Harold Watkins and his wife Catherine Beall Watkins, live in this two-story three bay farm house. The house has a gable roof with a center gable which has returned cornices and a widow. The front porch has been enclosed. This house has been in the Watkins family for over 120 years.

51. Barnes Farm

On the 1881 road plat this property belonged to Luther M. Browning. By 1900, James Oliver Barnes and Harriet Emma Day Barnes were living here, as indicated in the census. The house pictured below is two-story five bay with a gable roof, and gable facade which has a window. A balustrade ran the length of the porch on both floors. The five bedroom house was lost in a fire. The large bank barn, corn crib and a stone spring house, built by Samuel Shipley, remain. The house was conveyed to Herbert Edward Barnes and his wife Rosa May Lewis Barnes raised their family here.

52. Bennett House

At the time the 1891 road plat was drawn, Reuben Engle had a one-story log house on this property. Richard H. and Sybelle Browning Bennett purchased the farm and had the log house incorporated into the present two-story frame structure after 1881. The center gable has returned corners and an arched window. The full-length front porch roof is supported by ten bracketed posts on two sides of the house. There is a single brick end chimney. Sybelle Bennett left the farm to Raymond and Talmadge Bennett. After a land trade, the property became the home of Talmadge and Libby Beall Bennett in the 1940's. In 1968 Libby Bennett sold the property to Earl C. Smith.

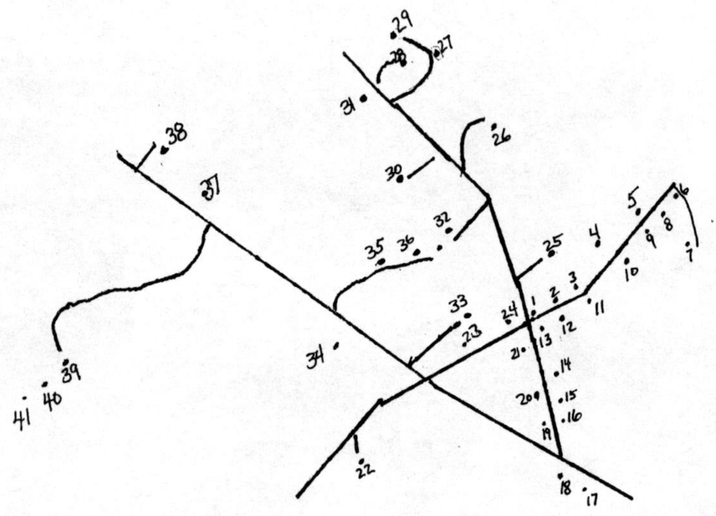


**Map of Lewisdale**

## THE HISTORY OF LEWISDALE

Lewisdale was founded by Alexander Lewis. It is located near the Montgomery - Frederick County line, between Browningsville, Purdum and Hyattstown. With the exception of Webb Beall's Store, the remaining historic buildings are residential structures. The rolling hills of the area are typical of this part of Maryland and many farms that dot the landscape have been in the same family for multiple generations. Prior to 1880 many of these farm's main crop was tabacco, however acreage planted in that crop steadily decreased until about 1919 when grains and dairy farming became prominent. This change was partly due to new roads in 1910, 1915 and 1920 which provided routes for farmers to get produce to markets. The crossroads of this rural, agricultural community contain several late nineteenth century and early twentieth century buildings.

Many of the lots in Lewisdale can be traced back to property that Margaret Lucinda Watkins Beall purchased from her father, Samuel B. Watkins, estate. Some of these lots were sold, and others were conveyed to her children between 1900 — 1918. One of these was Samuel Webster Beall, a merchant of Lewisdale.

Like neighboring communities Lewisdale had it's own band. The King's Select Band photograph dates to 1927 and from left to right are: Sam Browning, Sherman Mullinix, Urner Mullinix, Grant Watkins, Dick Gue, Clyde Lawson, Fillmore C. King, Gene Mullinix, Jesse "Dick" Day, Charles LaTona, Tobias Watkins, Ed Smith, Thurston "Jack" Brown, Jess Smith.

## Houses and Buildings in Lewisdale

1. Webb Beall's Store

The 1879 atlas shows David Snowden living here. Present building was constructed by Basil D. Schwartz in the 1897-8 for Samuel Webster Beall on property which he acquired from his mother, Margaret Lucinda Watkins Beall. The two-and-a-half story frame three bay building had a hall upstairs that was used for various gatherings. The general mercantile had everything from lamp oil to cloth, and groceries to shoes and was the focal point of activities. John Haines recalls attending a Branch Sunday School of Bethesda Methodist Church here in the 1930's. The photograph was taken 1906 and a poster for the Frederick Fair can be seen on the side of the building. Webb Beall is standing in the doorway with his twin daughters Hilda and Helena. His brother, Luther Chapman Beall, is seated on the white horse. The post office was located here, according to Helena Beall Lewis, when she was a child. (b. 1901). After Mr. Beall retired in the early 1920's, Hilda and Titus "Deets" Day operated the store. They operated the store until 1957, at which time it was leased to Bill Keith and subsequently Alvin Wayne "Juggs" Thompson. It was called the A & W store until when it went out of business in the 1981. The property is part of "Resurvey of Trouble Enough Indeed".

2. Webb Beall House

This two-story frame residence was built by Basil Dorsey Schwartz for Webb Beall on property purchased from Margaret L. Watkins Beall. The center gable has a window and the front porch runs the length of the house. Samuel Webster Beall lived over the newly built store while the house was under construction in 1899 and was married to Altie Everett King on July 11, 1900. Their twin daughters Hilda and Helena were born in August of 1901. The kitchen wing addition with an upstairs bedroom was constructed in 1919. Hilda was married on the front porch of the house to Titus "Deets" Day on October 26, 1922. Webb and Altie Beall lived here until the early 1950's. When Alvin Wayne Thompson was operating the store he lived here. Dominique Day lives here presently. The exterior walls have been covered with aluminum siding. The property is part of "Resurvey of Trouble Enough Indeed".

3. Beall - Duvall House

This two-story frame house was built for Winsor and Lula Tucker Beall after his mother, Margaret Lucinda Watkins Beall, conveyed the property to him. Mrs. Tucker, Lula's mother, lived with them. The house has a three bay facade, and a rear ell and front porch. One section of the porch has been enclosed. The remaining porch roof is suppored by turned bracketed posts with lattice under the porch. In each gable is an arched widow. The side gables have returned cornices and the gable roof is covered with shingles. The house was conveyed to Marguerite Beall Duvall daughter of Winsor Beall, wife of Olie Duvall. The property is part of the tract "Resurvey of Trouble Enough Indeed" and is now owned by their daughter, Louisa.

4. Marshall Beall House

This two-story five bay frame residence was built for Fillmore and Fannie Watkins Beall c. 1886 and sat on a 135 acre parcel of the Watkins farm. The house has Victorian influences and windows in the gable ends. The residence was built on a rock face stone foundation. The wooden porch, which runs the length of the facade was built on brick piers and has a low hipped roof. In 1905 Fillmore and Fannie moved to Browningsville and Paul Beall rented the house, as did E. Minor Burns. In 1929, the property was sold to Marshall and Zerah Shipley Beall. Their children were: Raymond Chapman Beall, Della Mae Doolin, Mary Louise Ballew, Dallas Marshall, E. Eileen Wolfe, and Rev. Jerry Beall. Approximately 11 acres were parceled for Roy Beall, and other parcels were sold off, leaving 72 acres in 1991. The addition is two-story two bay with a gabled roof and a large brick chimney. Since 1979 it has been owned by Rev. Jerry and Cheryl Beall. The house was remodeled to accomodate their daughter's family as well. The property is part of "Resurvey of Trouble Enough Indeed".

5. Watkins House

This land was part of "Resurvey of Trouble Enough Indeed", the property divided after the death of Samuel B. Watkins and sold in lots by Margaret Lucinda Watkins Beall. Bradley Watkins, a grandson of Samuel purchased the property and had the two-story frame house built c. 1897. It is five bay by one bay and has a gable roof. The facade has a center gable with returned cornices. The front porch roof is supported by turned posts on brick piers. The front door has side lights and a transom. Bradley Watkins and his wife Rebecca Zerah Burdette farmed here until he built a house on Bethesda Burch Road. The house was conveyed to their son-in-law after they moved to Browningsville. Charles Franklin Burdette and his wife Roberta Eveline Watkins Burdette lived here until his death in 1947. Mrs. Burdette then married Titus Brown.

6. Light Hill Schoolhouse

The Montgomery County Board of Education began a building program in 1865 in which Light Hill School was named as school #9. Located midway between Lewisdale and Browningsville, it served both communities at this time. In 1868 Charles W. Browning taught the spring semester and had 66 students enrolled. He also taught the fall semester that year and then Warner Wellington Welsh taught the 1869 spring semester. In the 1890's the school was thirty years old and received repairs and new furniture. The last two teachers here were Vernon D. Watkins and Arthur R. Watkins. In June of 1900 the school closed and students attended the Lewisdale School. Priscilla J. Beall Green, who owned the property up the lane, purchased the property for $100 in 1901. Her son Harry Green and his wife Ethel Mullinix Green lived here after the school was converted into a residence. It was purchased by Leroy and Irene Shipley Arnold and two of their daughters live here presently. The property was part of "Cecil's Chance".

Students of Light Hill School

7. Burdette-Beall Farm

This property was part of the James W. Burdette property. The two-story frame house was built c. 1890 for Luther and Effie W. Davis Burdette. Luther was a grandson of James W. Burdette. The farm was sold to William Chapman Beall and his wife Priscilla Jane Beall, a daughter of Caleb and Margaret Lucinda Watkins Beall. It has a main three bay section, center gabled roof and a rear two-story two bay ell forming a T-shape. The house has an open front porch and end stove chimneys. Priscilla Beall conveyed it to her son Jesse J. Beall in 1942. Jesse was married to Emma Mullinix Beall and had three children: Malcolm Beall, Willard Beall and Dorothy Beall. The property is part of "Trouble Enough."

8. Site of Beall - Musgrove House

This log house was built for the William A. Beall c. 1877 and was moved to Waterford, Virginia's Heritage Museum. After the death of his first wife, Anna M. Beall, he married Frances Virginia Watkins. Their fifth child, Nora, married Stanley Musgrove and they lived in another house behind the cabin in which James Page and his family had previously lived. In 1900 the lane went all the way to Purdum Road, passing the King farm. Another occupant of the log house was William's granddaughter, Esther Mae Thompson Hurley. The top photo shows Stanley and Nora Musgrove's family on the front porch. The lower photograph shows the house which was located near the large walnut tree. Mr. Bill Haines hauled the cabin to Virginia in 1963. A modern house is there now. The property was part of "Cecil's Chance".

9. Reece Mullinix House

Sherman Mullinix purchased this property and had the house built by Josh Musgrove, but subsequently sold it to his brother Reece and his wife, Julia E .Mullinix. They previously lived in a small cabin several doors up the road. The two-story three bay by one bay frame house has a gable roof with returned cornice and a center brick chimney. The porch roof is supported by turned posts and a balustrade around the house. The property is part of "Cecil's Chance". When Julia Mullinix died in 1962, the house was sold. After an interim owner, Kenny Shoemaker purchased the house and repaired it. Howard Haines was the subsequent owner. He sold it to Pedersen Henning, the present occupant.

10. Grimes House

This house is a two-story frame house with a three bay facade. It has a gable roof with a center gable facade. The front porch is supported by posts and an iron balustrade. The property is part of "Cecil's Chance". The house was built for Della and James Berman Grimes c. 1908. Their daughter Iris Grimes was born here in 1909. Turner J. Keith and his wife, Fannie C. Keith lived here after the Grimes family did. Their children were: William, Edward and Wesley Keith. Allen Burdette was a subsequent owner who had the addition constructed.

11. Watkins House

This was originally the site of a log house built for the Mullinix family. It was torn down and replaced by the frame house for Monroe and Mattie Watkins in 1918. Their daughter Ada lived here subsequently. The house is a two-story frame three bay structure with a gable roof. The facade has a center gable with window which has been closed in, and returned cornices. The front porch has been enclosed and the side entrance has a small porch. The house has been remodeled several times giving an ecclectic impression. The property is part of "Cecil's Chance". Debbie Haines and her family live here presently.

12. Dorsey Lewis House

The property was originally part of the Samuel B. Watkins farm, and was purchased by his daughter, Margaret Lucinda Watkins Beall when the farm was divided. The land was part of "Cecil's Chance" and was conveyed to Helena K. Beall Lewis in 1927 when her twin sister received the adjoining property. This residence is an example of the American Foursquare house and was built 1928 for Dorsey and Helena K. Beall Lewis. The hipped dormered roof typifies the style of house. The two-story frame two bay by two bay house has a front porch with a roof supported by four Doric columns. Dorsey Lewis worked for a local contractor and built many of the area barns. The Lewis's raised many foster children here and the house was sold after the death of Mr. Lewis in 1975 to Gregory P. and Patricia Fortez.

13. Day House

This property was part of the Samuel B. Watkins farm and was purchased by his daughter, Margaret Lucinda Watkins Beall. She sold this lot to Samuel Webster and Altie King Beall in 1927 who deeded it to their daughter, Hilda Beall Day. This is a parcel of the tract "Cecil's Chance." The house style is a variation on the bungalow house design which was covered in multi-colored broken peices of glass mixed with stucco and was built for Hilda and Titus Deets Day in 1927. It is a one-and-a-half story frame two bay by three bay residence. The charming dormers are set off by the center front facing gable. The gable ends are decorated with diamond and scalloped shaped shingles. Hilda Day lived here until her death in 1985, and then her sister Helena Beall Lewis lived here until her death in 1988. Presently Martha Day, wife of Winfred Day, lives here.

## 14. Lewis - Gue House

Alexander 'Hanson' Lewis was born in 1830 to Jeremiah and Mary Windsor Lewis. He married Emeline Burdette and had four children: Mary E., Emma J., Ida M., and Jeremiah Lewis. Hanson was one of the original Trustees for the Mountain View Church in Purdum. It was his son Jeremiah that ran the store in Lewisdale at the turn of the last century. This house was built around the time of Hanson's marriage in the mid-1850's. For many years the Gue family lived here followed by Sherman Mullinix who was first married to Annie Watkins, then Valinda C. Burdette Lewis. After her death he married Elsie Trout who had lived here with the Gue family. The property is part of "Trouble Enough". There is a family cemetery on the property. Mr. and Mrs. Duvall lived here in the 1940's and later the Welfare Department owned this house for a time and rented it out. More recently the house was owned by Gary Haines who remodeled it and then sold it.

15. Day House

One-story three bay by one bay frame house built by Titus Deets Day c.1930. This was the home of Jesse "Dick" Day and his wife Leanna Lewis Day until the mid-1950's. Their daughter, Mary Ann Day Raines was the subsequent owner. The gable roof extends to form the porch roof which is supoorted by posts, and the balustrade surrounds the porch. The property is part of "Trouble Enough".

16. Lewis-Day House

This house was built by Titus Deets Day c. 1930 for Vinnie and Lola Lewis. It is a rectangular three bay, one-story house with gable front facade. The property is part of "Trouble Enough". Other residents include Benny and Bessie White, Bill and Rosalie Huff, who operated the Purdum store and Winfred and Martha Ann Day. Winfred Day is the present owner and occupant.

17. Lewisdale Schoolhouse

The Lewisdale School was built for $350 in 1900. The land was purchased from Jeremiah Lewis for $40. The building was 22 X 34 feet, but by 1913 additional room was required. Space was rented until the addition could be added, which was a 30 X 30 one-story expansion. In 1921 the community requested high school subjects be offered at Lewisdale, but they were denied additional grades. In 1931 Velma Deason was the teacher. The school was closed in 1935 and the property was sold to Titus 'Deets' Day for $985. The school was converted into a residence for Mr. and Mrs. O'Neel and subsequently the Shifflet's lived here.

Lewisdale students in 1905: Front: Clyde Lawson, Ronald Beall, Elmer Gue, Lester Watkins, Maynard Watkins, Titus Deets Day, Henson Gue, Walter Lawson, Dolston Burdette. Second: Raymond Gue, Libby Beall, Myrtle Burns, Pauline Burdette, Clark Lewis, Delsie King, Ella Brown, Fannie Lewis, Clara Beall, Paul Beall, Roland Page, Lawrence Keith, Eugene Mullinix. Third: Myrtle Gue, Myrtle Day, Nora Beall, Rena Lewis, Rose Watkins, Pearl Watkins, Vernie Davis, Anna Lawson, Dorothy Lawson, Roby Watkins. Fourth: Mazie Watkins Day, Fannie Burdette, Bertha Lawson, Sallie King, Bell King, Hattie Watkins, Cora Watkins, Sara Elizabeth Lawson Beall, and teacher: Essie King. Back: John M. King, Cora Clark Burdette King, Perry Watkins, Urner Mullinix, Harry Beall, Barry Beall, Ivan Lawson.

Lewisdale students in 1917: Back Row: Alma B______, Nora King, Julia ____, Mrs. Barber. Second Row: Edna Burdette, _____ Grimes, Vertie Watkins, Gertrude Wolfe, Mamie Day. Third Row: Claudia Jamison, Julia Beall, ____ Howes, _____ Barnes, _____ Gue, Ollie Lewis, Marshall Beall. Fourth Row: Herbert Mullican, Silas Beall, Irving Gue, Jessie Day, W. Taft King, Jesse King, Jr. Seated: ____ Gue, ______, _______, Gene Lewis, Elwood Beall. Standing: Kits Gue, Edna Beall, _____ Mullican, _____ Gue and Ada Watkins.

Lewisdale students in 1931 Front Row: Otis Haines, Melvin Mullinix, Arthur Davis, Gene Hawes, Edward Beall, Helen Beall, Anna Burns Burdette. Second Row: Day Mullinix, Clark Davis, John Beall, William Haines, Lawrence Luhn, Ray Mullinix, Perry Lewis. Third Row: Rena Davis, Mildred Brown, Mary Mae Burns, Violet King, John Haines, Pearl Brown, Rudell Beall, Bernie Lewis. Fourth row: Ruth Davis, Maguartie Beall, Bernice Woodfile, Mary Mullinix, Ella Mullinix, Howard Beall. Back row: Walter Haines, Willard Smith, Harold Day.

18. Day House

This two-story frame house has a three bay facade and two exterior brick end chimneys. The two gabled dormers and roof are covered with raised seam metal. The porch has a shed roof supported by four posts. The house was built for Titus Deets Day and is now owned by Winfred Day. Various occupants have rented the house, including: James and Ruth Watkins, Alton and Doris Shipley and Lee and Mary Lou Beall Ballew.

19. Lewis's Store

This was the location of Jeremiah Lewis's store. The building is rectangular with a gable facade, center brick chimney, and the shed porch roof is supported by turned posts. His house was located next to the store, but it was destroyed by fire many years ago. Jeremiah married Valinda C. Burdette and they ran the store. He was also the first postmaster and the town was named after him. After his death, she married Sherman Mullinix who was the subsequent merchant. The store was later purchased by Titus Deets Day and converted into a house. It was rented to Maurice Shipley c. 1933, and being a carpenter, he added on to the back and side. Mr. Shipley married Nora Brown and they lived here until they moved to Damascus. This property is part of "Trouble Enough".

20. Tetlow House

This two-story frame house has a three bay facade with a gable roof. The center gable and roof are covered with raised seam metal. The gable has an arched window and returned cornice. The shed roof on the porch is supported by slightly tapered columns, and the foundation of the house is stone. The house was built for Albert G. Tetlow and his wife Dolly Tetlow. The subsequent residents were Gideon and Della Beall Doolan. This property is part of "Trouble Enough".

21. Mullinix House

This house was built for Urner R. and Emma Rena Lewis Mullinix. It is a two-story three bay by one bay frame house with a center brick chimney. The gable ends have returned cornices. The front porch has a shed roof supported by four posts. The foundation is of stone and the exterior is sheathed with siding. A subsequent owner was Ray Smith. This property is part of "Trouble Enough".

22. James Wilkerson Day House

This land was the property of William Simpson Beall in 1754. Basil Beall and Matilda Mark Beall's daughter Sarah Wilson Beall married James Wilkerson Day. The earlier house of Basil Beall burned and the present house was built for James Wilkerson Day in 1890. The two-and-a-half story frame five bay by one bay residence has a center gable and the front porch runs the length of the facade. The trim is of chestnut wood. Nephews Barry and Leslie Beall moved here in 1912. The bank barn was constructed in 1913 and was built from lumber cut on the farm. Dairying operation began in 1920 after local roads were improved to allow products to be sent to market. Behind the fields of this farm was a log house which belonged to Rebecca Norwood. The foundation is all that remains. This property is part of "Cecil's Chance".

23. Leslie Beall Farm

This property had long been in the Watkins, Day and Beall family. It was conveyed to Leslie Gordon Beall and Bessie Lewis Beall in 1918 after he and his brother, Barry Ranson Beall, had acquired forty-four acres between 1911 - 1916. The two-story three bay frame house has a gabled roof house and was built in 1921. Notice the cornice work in the center gable with the typical arched window. The farm became a dairy farm in the 1920's after roads were improved allowing farmers who were not along the B & O railroad access to markets by truck. Their son, Rudell Carroll Beall, was the subsequent owner. The dairy barn is just out of the picture to the left. The present owners, Charles and Robert Beall, recently had the gazebo added to the front porch. The property is part of "Resurvey on Trouble Enough Indeed".

24. Schwartz - Watkins House

This two-story frame residence is three bay by one bay, has a gable roof and a brick chimney. It was built in 1900 by Basil D. Schwartz who married Pink Priscilla Piquette in October of 1900. This quarter acre of property was purchased from Margaret Lucinda Watkins Beall in July of 1900. Mr. Schwartz was a carpenter, and built the two-story board and batten structure for his carpenter shop. In September, 1919 Basil and Pink Schwartz sold the house to C. Fillmore and Jemima C. Lewis. The rear addition with first floor kitchen was added about this time. The seven room house was sold for $1,850 in 1937 to Roby Selman and Margaret Catherine Runkles Watkins. Mr. Watkins enlarged the shop and used it for his automobile work. The welding shop faces Price's Distillery Road and the barn is just out of the photo to the left. The present owners are Carl and Vinnie Lewis. The property is part of "Resurvey on Trouble Enough Indeed".

25. Roy Beall House

Leroy Beall, son of Caleb and Margaret Lucinda Watkins Beall, received a portion of their farm in 1929. To this was added some acreage previously owned by Filmore and Fannie Beall. Roy Beall had this American Four-square house built. It has a two bay facade and a brick chimney. The facade has a single dormer and window. The porch has a hipped roof supported by four columns. The property is owned by Nelson Beall, son Monroe Beall. He had the wing addition constructed. Nelson Beall owns Beall's Bulldozing Company and lives here presently. The property is part of "Resurvey on Trouble Enough Indeed".

26. Samuel B. Watkins Farm

The property which formed Samuel B. Watkins' holdings were purchased from several owners, beginning in 1834 with acreage from Mary J. Thomas. In 1841 he bought from Joseph Nichollson, from Joseph Watkins in 1850, and from James Henderson in 1874. The older section of the house was constructed of logs and was one story. When the two-story three bay by two bay addition was built the exterior brick chimney became a central chimney, between the two sections. The log corn crib is on a stone foundation, as is the barn. After Samuel B. Watkins' death in 1885 the eight children inherited 642 1/2 acres. Part was from the tract "Adams Choice" and part was from "Resurvey on Trouble Enough Indeed". Because the property was not easily divided, it was sold by a trustee. At that time there were three dwellings and a number of out buildings and the property extended to both sides of Price's Distillery Road. The farm was purchased by Julius and Amanda Watkins and they raised their children here: Tobias, Sam, Grant, Fannie, Mae, Monroe, Etta, Hattie, Cora, Ed and Annie. Ernest H. King married Hattie G. Watkins King and lived here subsequently. The property was later sold and a new house was built by the current owner, John R. Meiklejohn.

27. Watkins Farm

This was the home of James Watkins and Addie Shipley Watkins. They purchased the property c. 1911. The rural vernacular frame house had a rear addition with a wrap around porch. The side of the house is pictured below with Addie Shipley Watkins in the center of the photograph. The house is no longer standing, but was located on the lane to Beall's Florist shop, off Price's Distillery Road.

28. Ed Beall Farm

Located on Price's Distillery Road, Ed Beall's farm was parceled from the adjoining Beall property. In 1877 Caleb Asbury Beall and his wife Margaret Lucinda Watkins Beall moved here with their children. The house was, at that time, a two story chestnut log dwelling. Luther Beall acquired the house and with his wife Della Mae Beall, added to the log portion of the house. Marshall and Zerah B. Shipley Beall lived here with his parents for a short a few years before moving to their farm. Presently Raymond Beall and his wife Marie L. Thatcher Beall own in the L shaped farm house, which has a three bay facade with a center gable extended by arch windows and returned cornice. In the photograph the large bank barn is visible with the Basil Beall farm behind it. Tenants presently occupy the house.

29. Basil Beall Farm

The two-story log section of the house was built before the Beall family purchased the property in 1771 from John Johnson. The farm is presently made up of four tracts: "Miller's Grove", "Ebony Marsh", "Resurvey of Johnson's Chance" and "Partnership". Basil was married to Sarah Mark in 1819, and following her death remarried. They lived in the log portion of the house, pictured below in the rear of the structure. Following Basil's death in 1875 his eldest son Richard Cronin Beall, inherited the farm. He married Sarah Elizabeth Lawson in 1885 and raised his family here. His son Silas Cronin Beall operated the farm beginning in the 1930's. Silas brought produce to the markets in Washington, and invited the author's great-grandfather up many times to fill his trunk with corn. His son Danny Beall and wife Christine presently operate Beall's Florist here and have several green houses on the property. Thus the farm has been in the family over 150 years. The house is now sheathed with weatherboarding. The house has been remodeled several times.

30. Lewis - Haines Farm

The one-story log section of the house was built by John R. Lewis c. 1848. The second section of the house was built by William Filmore Lewis for c. 1878 at the time of his first marriage to Laura Belle King. After her death he married Olive M. Watkins. The chimney was part stone and part brick. Walter Edward Haines and his wife Rosie Mabel Smith Haines were the subsequent owners. The front porch had collapsed before this photograph was taken in the 1970's. A modern house has was built on the farm by Walter Edward Haines. The property is part of "Resurvey on Wildcat Spring".

31. Samuel C. Watkins House

This was the home of Samuel Cummings Watkins and his wife Josephine Lee Watkins. There were married c. 1898 and the house dates to that time. The facade had four bays and a gable roof. The center brick chimney provided heat for the house. In 1929 a full-length front porch was added. Samuel Calvin Watkins was born here in 1905 and married Nettie Emily Burdette in 1929. The house was purchased by Howard Haines in the 1950's. It is no longer standing, and modern houses are on the site of the farm.

32. Tobias Watkins House

This property is part of "Resurvey on Wildcat Spring". The home is a two-story five bay by one bay frame house presently covered with asbestos siding. The gable roof is covered with raised seam metal and the gable facade has an arched window. The double brick chimneys provide heat to the large house. The foundation is stone. A side porch has a shed roof supported by four turned posts and the front porch is presently a gable roof addition. The house is presently owned by Rudell Beall. A tenant house is in the overgrowth between the field of Tobias and Joseph Grant Watkins houses. It is a two-story three bay frame house with raised seam metal roof and shed roof over the porch which runs the length of the facade. It is presently unoccupied but once was the home of Francis C. and Cordelia A. Beall.

33. Watkins - Beall House

This was the home of Edward E. Watkins and Cordelia B. Mullinix. The house was built c. 1890 and Edward died in 1900. Cordelia then married Oscar Thomas Mullican. The property was part of "Resurvey on Wildcat Spring". The attractive two-and-a-half story frame house has Victorian influences in trim and design. The typical center gable has an arched window and the porch has been enclosed. The three bay by one bay house has had three additions, with an exterior chimney on the west end. Pearl Watkins Beall, daughter of the original owners lived here and married Fletcher T. Beall. Carl Oscar Mullican and his wife Helen Mildred Day Mullican also lived here. The farm is now owned by Rudell Beall and is rented to his grandson, Kevin Beall. After the barn was destroyed by fire, it was replaced by a metal barn.

34. Titus W. Day House

This was the farm of Titus Washington Day and Rosa B. King Day. The property is part of "Resurvey on Wild Cat Spring". The original section of the house was built c. 1897 and is a frame two-story three bay by two bay house with two interior chimneys. The steep center gable with pattern shingles has an arched window and the front porch is supported by four columns. The rear two-story ell has an exterior chimney with two additions beyond. The log tobacco house and frame bank barn remain in good condition. Other occupants include Robert and Mary Ann Beall, Kevin and Rose Beall and Rudell Carroll Beall lives here presently.

35. Hawes House

This house was built c. 1900 and is a two-story frame three bay by one bay with gable roof. The roof is covered in corrugated metal with a center gable facade. The center gable has a single window and shed roof porch is supported by four posts. It was built for James Columbus and Gertrude E. B. Hawes and their family. The house has been abandoned for many years and a modern house has been built beside it. The property is a parcel of "Resurvey on Wild Cat Spring".

36. Joseph Grant Watkins House

The property for this farm came from "Resurvey of Wild Cat Spring". The front section of this house is log, and has been restored recently. The two-story addition was built of frame and several of the outbuildings remain. Joseph Grant Watkins and Nettie F. Beall Watkins are the parents of Lester Steele Watkins who married Mazie Nadine Brandenburg Watkins. Presently the Leef family is living here.

37. Haines Farm

James S. Haines married Gertrude F. Nichols in 1885 and built this two story frame house. The original section is three bay by one bay and had two brick chimneys. The two-story addition also has a brick chimney. The gable roof has a center gable facade with a window. The front porch runs the length of the original house and is supported by posts. The rear porch has been enclosed. The road beside the house, Haines Road, was named for the orignal owners. In 1943 the house was destroyed by fire and John Haines rebuilt the house exactly as it had been before the fire. Since that time an addition has been constructed.

38. Thompson Farm

Mrs. Ellen Thompson owned this farm and left it to her grandson, Joseph Douglas Thompson, who married Ella Nora Thompson of Thompson's Corner. They lived in the log house until 1900 when they had the present house built. Their 13 children were born here and their son Horace Melvin Thompson farmed here. He married Lula M. Bennett Thompson and raised two daughters, Mary and Barbara here. Athough the blacksmith shop is no longer standing, the location is still remembered by Horace's daughters. Lindy and Ruth Beall lived here in the 1950's. The front porch was removed by a subsequent owner, Jesse Aiken, who also sold off the fields where new houses were built behind the farm. The present owner is Charles Stouffer. The barn to the left of the house was built in 1908. The property was a parcel of "Cecil's Chance".

39. Charles Browning Farm

This property was parceled from Joshua Cecil's property "Cecil's Chance". The two-story house was built for Charles T. Browning and his wife Mary Jane King Browning c. 1860. In 1900 John P. Harris owned the house and was living here with his niece Bertie J. Bell. He was a widower, and re-married in 1906. Later occupants were Ernest Walter Mullican, Maynard and Edna Kling, and then Willis and Dot Beall rented the farm from Mr. Patterson. There are number of outbuildings which are well preserved. The Little Bennett Golf Course meanders over the former farm acreage. Jeremiah Norwood lived in a log house nearby, but it is no longer standing. Other homes in the area included those of Charles Miles, Charles W. Shern, Robert L. Gray, George K. Brandenburg and William Hackey.

39. John N. Soper House

The older log section of the house was one-and-a-half stories with a chimney. The second section was two-story frame with a stone chimney. The interior had plastered walls with chair rails and baseboards. The stairs were boxed stairs in the corner. 1900 lists this farm as #139 and John is listed as born in 1818, owns mortgaged farm, living with him are brothers Ruben B. Soper, 1824, farm laborer, Samuel 1837, farm laborer, and sister Susan J. 1826, keeps house. Between the Soper house and the Thompson farm was a home which is now gone. At the turn of the twentieth century it was the home of Nathan Keith, and his family, who farmed here. Both were parcels of "Resurvey on Wild Cat Spring".

40. Cecil-Perry Browning House

The log house was built for Joshua Cecil, c. 1751. A subsequent owner was Perry Browning, who had an addition built. When the house was sheathed with siding additonal windows were cut into the cabin walls. Joseph Melvin Burdette lived here and farmed in the 1930's and 1940's. The Smith's lived here in the 1960's. The house is now inhabited by golf course maintaince personnel and is enclosed by a chain link fence. The property was called "Resurvey on Wild Cat Spring".

## Bibliography


A Grateful Remembrance, Richard K. MacMaster and Ray Eldon Hiebert, 1976
Atlas of Montgomery County, Maryland, C. E. Hopkins, 1879
Civil War Guide to Montgomery County, Maryland, Charles T. Jacobs, MCHS, 1983
County Courier, "Salute to Clarksburg-Past and Present," Martha Klopper
Damascus Courier-Gazette, "Clarksburg Colored School Remembered," Jill Teunis February 24, 1993
Damascus Gazette, "Mendelsshon Terrace Farm," Jill Teunis, April 5, 2000
Diary of Ruth Buxton Dowden, 1909
The History of Bethesda United Methodist Church, Bernardine Gladhill Beall, 1988
The History of Clarksburg United Methodist Church, Ralph Fraley Martz, 1953
The History of Frederick County, Vol. II, T. J. C. Williams and Folger McKinsey, 1910, L. R. Titsworth
The History of Hyattstown, D. Cuttler and Mike Dwyer, Heritage Books, Inc., 1998
The History of Kingsley School, Mark Walston, unpublished manuscript, 1979
The History of Montgomery County, Maryland by Thomas H. Stockton Boyd, Clarksburg, Md., 1879
The History of Mountain View Methodist Church, Richie Lee Hainey
The History of Western Maryland, Thomas Scharf, 1882
Interviews with Mary Lou Beall Ballew, D. Cuttler, 1999-2001
Interview of Betty Mae King Barton, D. Cuttler, March 2001
Interview of Betty Mae King Barton, Eloise Haney Woodfield, April, 2001
Interviews with Bernardine Gladhill Beall, D. Cuttler 1999-2000
Interview of Zerah Shipley Beall, Mary Lou Beall Ballew, March, 2001
Interview of Zerah Shipley Beall, D. Cuttler, June 2000
Interview Harold Bennett, D. Cuttler, March, 2001
Interviews with Elizabeth Miles Burdette, 1998-2000, D. Cuttler
Interview of Anice Julia Murphy Cecil, Lawrence Cecil, 1980
Interview of Ann Continetti, Eloise Haney Woodfield, April, 2001
Interviews with Anice Lee Cecil Dancy, D. Cuttler, 1996-2000
IInterview of Dorothy Day, Mark Walston, July 1979
Interview of Helena Beall Day, Michael Dwyer, 1974
Interview of Patricia Denu, D. Cuttler, March, 2001
Interview of Patricia Denu, Eloise Haney Woodfield, April, 2001
Interview of Katherine Ricketts Dronenburg, Mark Walston, July 1979
Interview of Buck Gladhill, D. Cuttler, June, 2000
Interview of Ethel Scott Gladhill, D. Cuttler, June, 2000
Interview of John Glaze, Bernardine Gladhill Beall, June, 2000
Interview of John Glaze, Eloise Haney Woodfield, March, 2000
Interviews of Virginia Hackey Gray, D. Cuttler, April and June, 2000
Interview of Elsie Pearson Green, Mark Walston, June 1979
Interview of Marjorie Green, D. Cuttler, March 2001
Interview of George Hackey, D. Cuttler, June, 2000
Interview of Howard Haines, Eloise Haney Woodfield, April, 2001

Interview of Ruth E. Watkins Haines, Ritchie Lee Haney, March 2001
Interview of Esther King Haney, D. Cuttler, April, 2000
Interview of Esther King Haney, Eloise Haney Woodfield, March, 2001
Interview of Esther King Haney, Mark Walston, June, 1979
Interview of Irvin Hurley, Ritchie Lee Haney, March, 2001
Interview of Kenneth Thurston King, Bernardine Gladhill Beall, June, 2000
Interview of Kenneth Thurston King, Eloise Haney Woodfield, April, 2001
Interview of Ray Luhn, Ritchie Lee Haney, April, 2001
Interviews with Mary Beth McDonough, D. Cuttler, 1998-2001
Interview of Jack McDonough, D. Cuttler, June, 2000
Interview of Louisa Lewis Magruder, D. Cuttler, June, 2000
Interview of Henry Miles, D. Cuttler, 1999 - 2000
Interview of Delma Hood Mullineaux, July 1979, Mark Walston
Interview of Almeada Hilton Norwood, D. Cuttler, June 2000
Interview of Lorraine Purdum, Eloise Haney Woodfield, March, 2001
Interview of Alice Leighton Schmidt, Eloise Haney Woodfield, March, 2001
Interview of W. Frank Soper, D. Cuttler, June, 2000
Interview of Eunice Evelyn Burdette Walker, D. Cuttler, April, 2001
Interview of Stewart E. Walker III, D. Cuttler, April 2001
Interview of Harold Watkins, D. Cuttler, March, 2001
Interview of Phyllis Thompson Watkins, D. Cuttler, March, 2001
Interview with Colleen Murphy Wilcoxen, D. Cuttler, 1996
Interview of Wilson Wims, D. Cuttler, June, 2000
Interview of Gloria King Winter, D. Cuttler, April, 2001
Interview of Gloria King Winter, Eloise King Haney Woodfield, March, 2001
Interviews with Eloise Haney Woodfield, D. Cuttler, 2001
Interviews with Joann Snowden Woodson, D. Cuttler, 1999-2001
Interview of Joann Woodson, Eloise Haney Woodfield, April, 2001
James Day and His Descendants, Jackson Day, 1976
Map of Montgomery County, Maryland, Martenet and Bond, Philadelphia, 1865
Maryland National Capitol Park and Planning Commission, Clarksburg Historic District, Michael Dwyer, Gail Rothrock, Margaret Coleman, and Kevin Parker, 1979
Montgomery Circuit Records, D. Cuttler, 2000, Heritage Books, Inc.
Montgomery County Atlas, Hopkins, 1879, Philadelphia
Montgomery County Census, 1850, Bill Hurley, Heritage Books, Inc
Montgomery County Census, 1860, Bill Hurley, Heritage Books, Inc.
Montgomery County Census, 1870, Bill Hurley, Heritage Books, Inc.
Montgomery County Census, 1880, Bill Hurley, Heritage Books, Inc.
Montgomery County Census, 1900, Dona Cuttler, unpublished manuscript
Montgomery County Census, 1910, Dona Cuttler, unpublished manuscript
Montgomery County Census, 1920, Dona Cuttler, unpublished manuscript
Montgomery County Historical Society Library, File on Clarksburg
Montgomery County Land Records, BS 6: 257
Montgomery County Land Records, BS 10: 392
Montgomery County Land Records, EBP 2: 552

Montgomery County Land Records, EBP 13: 67
Montgomery County Land Records, EBP 6: 43
Montgomery County Land Records, EBP 7: 383
Montgomery County Land Records, EBP 8: 395
Montgomery County Land Records, EBP 8: 456
Montgomery County Land Records, EBP 11:268
Montgomery County Land Records, EBP 17: 221
Montgomery County Land Records, EBP 18: 24
Montgomery County Land Records, EBP 18: 187
Montgomery County Land Records, EBP 27: 380
Montgomery County Land Records, EBP 30: 435
Montgomery County Land Records, EBP 78: 235
Montgomery County Land Records, HGC 23: 344
Montgomery County Land Records, JA 3: 652
Montgomery County Land Records, JA 4: 446
Montgomery County Land Records, JA 7: 24
Montgomery County Land Records, JA 11: 247
Montgomery County Land Records, JA 38: 179
Montgomery County Land Records, JGH 2: 77
Montgomery County Land Records, JGH 2: 354
Montgomery County Land Records, JGH 5: 614
Montgomery County Land Records, JGH 6: 570
Montgomery County Land Records, K: 148
Montgomery County Land Records, L: 39
Montgomery County Land Records, N: 387
Montgomery County Land Records, Q: 187
Montgomery County Land Records, S-19: 404
Montgomery County Land Records, STS 4: 372
Montgomery County Land Records, T: 427
Montgomery County Land Records, TD 6:80
Montgomery County Land Records, TD 6: 243
Montgomery County Land Records, TD 12: 39
Montgomery County Land Records, TD 14: 494
Montgomery County Land Records, TD 16: 199
Montgomery County Land Records, TD 16: 200
Montgomery County Land Records, TD 22: 51
Montgomery County Land Records, TD 22: 229
Montgomery County Land Records, TD 22: 233
Montgomery County Land Records, TD 24: 439
Montgomery County Land Records, U: 121
Montgomery County Land Records, U: 295
Montgomery County Land Records, 104: 485
Montgomery County Land Records, 178: 143
Montgomery County Land Records, 203: 93
Montgomery County Land Records, 226: 357

Montgomery County Land Records, 230: 28
Montgomery County Land Records, 236: 212
Montgomery County Land Records, 257: 168
Montgomery County Land Records, 272: 374
Montgomery County Land Records, 362: 42
Montgomery County Land Records, 378:53
Montgomery County Land Records, 396: 424
Montgomery County Land Records, 556: 175
Montgomery County Land Records, 562: 124
Montgomery County Land Records, 634: 366
Montgomery County Land Records, 1077: 15
Montgomery County Land Records, 1537: 325
Montgomery County Map of 1865, Hopkins, 1865, Philadelphia
Rocky Hill School Roster, Joann Snowden Woodson, Ethel Foreman, Frances Wims Foreman, Robert Leroy Foreman and Arthur Randolph
Schools That Were, E. Guy Jewell, unpublished manuscript, 1979
Sentinel, "Early Days of Clarksburg," Ralph Fraley Martz, March 23 & 30, 1950
Sentinel, "The Old Clarksburg Band," Ralph Fraley Martz, 1960
Sentinel, "Trustees' Sale" June 12, 1903
Store Ledger of Beverly Waugh, 1815, Lovely Lane Museum, Baltimore, Md.
Store Ledger of John Clark(e), 1817, MCHS collection
Store Ledger of Ritchie E. Haney, 1943, Eloise Haney Woodfield collection
Store Ledger of Samuel Hobbs, 1910, The Walker Family collection
Two Centuries of Change, "The Montgomery County Sentinel," Ralph Martz September 21, 1954
Washington Star, "Never Say Die," by Lurma Rackley, May 24, 1947
Will of John Clark, Liber E, folio 9, 1802
Will of Joseph Burnside, Liber I folio 444, 1816
Zoning Actions Threaten Dairy Farming, "Gaithersburg Gazette," Ginny Earnshaw, April 15, 1983

# INDEX

Dona L. Cuttler is a Maryland native who descended from several pre-colonial Maryland family lines. She is a graduate of Takoma Academy, and USC, and presently is a public school music education specialist. Her great-grandfather and grandmother started the family interest in genealogy, and local history, and Ms. Cuttler has expanded the project throughout several counties in Maryland. This is the 9th book offered by Ms. Cuttler.